QUICK STORIES & POEMS VOL. 3

José F. Nodar, Publisher

Camden Books Spring Farm NSW Australia 2570

Copyright © 2025 by José F. Nodar

All rights reserved. No part of this publication may be reproduced, distributed, or transmitted in any form or by any means, including photocopying, recording, or other electronic or mechanical methods, without the prior written permission of the publisher, except in the case of brief quotations embodied in critical reviews and certain other non-commercial uses permitted by copyright law. The copyright of this publication is owned by José F. Nodar. The individual authors keep copyright of the individual stories/poetry.

Publisher's Note: This is a work of fiction. Names, characters, places, and incidents are a product of the author's imagination. Locales and public names are sometimes used for atmospheric purposes. Any resemblance to actual people, living or dead, or to businesses, companies, events, institutions, or locales is completely coincidental.

Quick Stories & Poems Vol. 3/ José F. Nodar. -- 1st ed.

ISBN 978-1-7643409-9-1 - Paperback

ISBN 978-1-7643714-0-7 - E-book

DEDICATION

To our family, our friends, the individual authors in this book, we appreciate your support.

FORWARD

This collection of short stories and poetry is the work of amazing authors who have taken the time to write a story or a poem to bring the reader into their lives.

The idea for this book was simple.

Let authors write and readers read.

I hope you enjoy the variety of stories/poetry in this book.

We thank you for your purchase and support.

ACKNOWLEDGEMENTS

As the publisher of this book, I would like to acknowledge all those authors, friends, and acquaintances who have had important roles in my life, which inspired me throughout my life.

To the individual authors who have trusted me with their work and allowed this book to be created. Thank you for your trust.

To my wife, my life is everything with you.

NOTES

Each author has certified:

He/she is eighteen years of age.

He/she has taken responsibility for all information in his / her stories/poetry.

The author knows this Publisher will not alter the wording of the story to make any corrections. Any error is the responsibility of the author.

The author may have received compensation for the use of their story/poetry.

To our readers, be mindful that the authors write using British, American, or Australian English, hence some words might look different.

Table of Contents

My Love 1

Talking With The Moon 7

In The Door 11

Airports, Aliens, And Time Warps 18

Whispers In The Wind 25

The Dreamscaper's Harvest 33

The Stranger 38

The Raven 47

Unconscious Writings 49

Love Serendipity 56

The Chin 58

Futures Hence 60

Deafening Cries 80

Quantum Physics And Gassed Cats 82

The Gazebo 92

Seven Days Of Pick Me Ups 97

A Hunter In The Wilderness 100

When There Is A Will There Is A Way 103

First Decision 108

It Cuts Deep	120
The Unseen	122
About My Sight	132
Threads	134
Epicurus The Buddha	139
Into The Waterfall	143
About The Authors	152

MY LOVE

―――――∞―――――

The first thing she thought was that no one would laugh at her again. The second thing, that perhaps she had made a mistake.

Twelve hours before

She looked at the foundations of her future house, clung to her fiancé's arm, trying to contain her joy, and felt like the luckiest woman in the world. She had never had too much, nor wanted more than she could have. Her world centred on Noah and the family project they talked about almost daily. It wouldn't be long until they were married and had their house finished, but she swore that she couldn't be happier than she was right now. And perhaps her life would prove her right.

"You are going to be the queen of this castle," he told her and kissed her on the forehead.

"And you are going to be the king, my love," Sofia responded, caressing his cheek.

Both the reader and I know that not everything is rosy and that there is no perfect couple. And this pair was about to find out. Unfortunately for Sofia, or for Noah, her fairy tale would transform into a horror story.

That night, they had gone out to dinner to celebrate and had a little too much. So much so that they had to return to the apartment they were renting by taxi. They entered the building stumbling and tempted to laugh, but one silenced the other so that later they wouldn't have to endure complaints from the neighbours. They entered their apartment, 4 C, and burst into laughter, although they no longer remembered what the joke was.

"I'll wait for you in bed," he warned her, wiping away the tears that escaped with his last laugh.

Sofia went to the kitchen to get a glass of water when she felt that her purse, which was still hanging from her shoulder, was vibrating. She opened it, took out her phone, but she still felt the vibration and she remembered that in the taxi, Noah had given her his to keep. She pulled out the second phone and a voicemail icon blinked on the screen. Without thinking twice, she went to take him to her fiancé, but she found him fast asleep, with half his body on the bed and his legs hanging over the side. She tried to wake him up but couldn't, so she lifted his legs as much as she could so that he would be more comfortable; Apparently, he wasn't even going to find out.

She watched him sleep and looked at the phone in her hand. Who was calling h im at 1 AM and for what? She wanted to listen to the message, but she realized that Noah had the phone locked, which surprised and bothered her in equal measure. She tried a couple of random passwords with no luck and then she remembered that he used to use the year of his birth in things like that. She tried it and when she put in the last number... Bingo!

The screen unlocked instantly.

She sat on the bed next to him and felt like she was doing something wrong, but the alcohol was still running through her body, and she couldn't think too much. She tapped the notification icon and listened to the voicemail instructions and the recording reciting the contact number, until she could finally hear the message: "Noah," a hesitant woman's voice could be heard, "I don't know how to tell you this, but..."

His breathing was laboured and Sofía's too due to expectation. "Today I took the test," she sobbed, "and it is positive. I'm pregnant".

Upon hearing that last word, Sofía felt as if she had been slapped, which sobered her instantly and at the same time she felt her body go limp as if it were made of jelly. She fell to the floor next to her bed, and her phone slipped from her shaking, cold hand. A thousand thoughts passed through her mind every second. She felt overwhelmed. Every limb of her body was trembling, and she felt like she didn't have the strength to get up. Tears fell down her cheeks and the cold sweat she felt on the back of her neck warned her of a possible fainting.

In a minute, her world was destroyed. Her past and her present were a lie; a lie that erased their much-desired future together in one fell swoop. The family they once desired, he would have with another. She remembered each of the moments with Noah and how his love for her was evident in each of them. She couldn't understand how he could have fooled her... especially now.

He had cheated on her. He had laughed at her and ruined her life.

She got up, dizzy, as best she could. She looked at his face and didn't recognize him. The one who slept peacefully while she was dying inside, now seemed like a stranger to her. A despicable man. She began to think about how, when and where he could have cheated on her... and how many times. And a spiral of dark thoughts was created in her mind. So dark that it led her to grab her pillow and press it over Noah's face. She squeezed as hard as she could; even a little more when he woke up and tried to get away, but it was too late. Within seconds, Noah's body went limp. He lay in bed with Sofia on top of him crying inconsolably, still clutching the pillow.

She was on him for so long that she lost count. Looking out the window, she saw that the night was beginning to give way to a new day.

What has she done!? What was she going to do?!

She tried to think quickly. Noah wouldn't ruin her life twice. She wouldn't go to prison because of him.

She grabbed his feet and began to pull with all her might until she managed to move him. It was not easy. He was tall and stocky. But Sofía was out of her mind and used all her strength to drag him to the bathroom. The hardest thing was getting him into the bathtub. Once she had him there, she filled it with water and pushed him under the water until his body was half his face submerged.

The first part was already done. But she needed to recreate the perfect scene. Her mind was going a million miles a minute.

She searched the apartment for all the alcohol she could find. She drank two cans of beer and grabbed an open wine and took it to the bathroom. She filled a glass and set it next to the bottle next to the bathtub. Then, she hurried to the bedroom, adjusted the covers on Noah's side, and lay down on her half of the bed. Even though she tried, she couldn't fall asleep. She waited like that, almost without moving, for two hours. When the sun came through the window and illuminated the room, she knew it was time for the last part.

She began to recreate the voicemail in her mind and the desperation, anguish and crying were instantly present. Using those emotions, she called the police and said that she had found her fiancé dead in the bathtub.

Two days later she was at the funeral of the person who was the great love of her life. She didn't need to pretend; she was truly devastated. If only he had behaved like the man he showed himself to be, their lives would be different now.

She was surrounded by people, but she couldn't see anyone. She did not want to. She was sitting in a corner, crying, when she heard the sobs of another woman whose voice she instantly recognized.

She followed the voice and stared at the woman hugging Noah's brother.

"Last night I called him to tell him that he was going to be an uncle," she heard the brunette say. "I left a voice message... he would have been so happy for us."

For the second time in a few hours, Sofia's heart skipped a beat. Her crying turned into desperate screams that caught the attention of everyone present, who felt sorry for her. For a murderer.

Mariela Ivón Armando © 2024

TALKING WITH THE MOON

This is a poem I wrote based on a writing prompt wherein the writer has to write a few lines around the theme of the old Gaelic proverb "The world will end but love and music will endure!"

She was sitting at the window,
looking at the stars,
counting each one, by one
wondering how far they are…

She happened to look at the moon
which suddenly spoke to her like a sister,
The moon said, 'What troubles you my child?',
She smiled and replied to the moon

"I want much more than this provincial life"
The moon replied
"let me tell you that your mother,
had said something similar to me as a young girl
she also talked to me freely, so I told her

José F. Nodar

If You Wish To Be Blamed, Marry;
If you wish to be praised, Die
Did you know It takes this much courage
for the moon to be a hope for others in the sky?

Trust me I the moon, do know why,
So continue like a wildflower
to be free, to have your own meaning,
to cast a light instead of a shadow…

To desire to be remembered, and to stand out alone,
like me as a beacon of hope, to cause a stir,
And not be one in the muck, who is always rather stuck,
But be the one who paints the path ahead
with one's own wisdom

When the whole world is drowning
in the sea of seeming confusion
(as if they too are lost in melodies
of their own choices and experiences)

Be all that you are-
because you have managed to come this far;
Be still, and know that you my friend,
are an immortal diamond of much worth in the sand…

When the young girl,
was done talking to the moon,
she looked at her phone and soon-
there was a text from her big sister Bex…

"Come to stay with me,
here in London, for eternity..
I know there in the desert,
its lonely too,
but here where I am,

There's real hope waiting for you…"
To which she replied
"Coming sis,
coz the moon gave me some advice-
about life that I never want to miss"

Then she sent her an emoji kiss
And prayed to God in earnest
She thought this could be the start of something new
Or the dreams of the night and more writing too

Writing about what made her smile,

Writing about what blessed her life,

Writing about prosperity too

Writing about the moon and how

it thought of me and raised an eyebrow

and said to its self "Even if this world ends,

Love wins, and so will you win my child"

So keep writing the story of your life

The world will end, but love and music will endure!

Believe and you will find your way…

Sarah Desouza © 2025

IN THE DOOR

———∞———

DI Ken Upchurch was sitting in the open doorway of a small Cessna 182 plane. Time had slowed down, he knew, at a conscious level, that he had only been there a few seconds, but it felt a lot longer than that. His left foot was on a very small steel step and his right foot was dangling over the edge.

While time seemed to be dragging slowly, his mind was running a fast chyron over the surreal experience.

'You're sitting in the open door of a plane, 2 miles above the ground and you're not wearing a parachute.'

Across from him, hanging onto the wing strut, grinning from ear to ear, and with her right foot perched on the same step was his girlfriend of three months, Plaid.

'She looks good Ken, a natural, but did you know that you're sitting in the open doorway of a Cessna 182, and you're not wearing a parachute.'

She flashed him a thumbs up and he must have seen it, because he made one back, but how, how could he give a thumbs up in this situation.

'But, remember, you are wearing a man called Art, who told you that he does this all the time. He gave you instructions, remember?'

Suddenly a hand appeared over his shoulder, and there was a camera attached to it, He saw it in his peripheral vision, because his eyes were still fixed on Plaid, who looked super keen to let go of the strut. Art's other hand turned his head, quite forcefully, to look at the camera and he heard the word "Ready?" shouted in his ear.

'You're not really ready, are you? But you can't back out, with your girlfriend grinning at you. She looks good in her pink and tartan jumpsuit doesn't she? Is she worth dying for though?'

To Ken, it felt like he'd been in the door of the plane for at least 5 minutes, but in reality it was about 5 seconds. The chyron in his mind kept scrolling, and he felt himself nodding. Had he done that voluntarily or did Art manipulate his head. It was Art, pulling his head back, what had he been told to do. His arms were crossed over his chest. Was that right? Wasn't he supposed to put them out sometime? When was that? He could not remember for the life of him, what he was supposed to do.

'For the life of you, that's very apt Ken, maybe reconsider that phrase?'

As his head was being pulled back he noticed Plaid making an in and out gesture with her arm, what was she trying to tell him? Was she gesturing to him or to Art? What was he supposed to do? Then he heard it.

"ARCH!" and they rocked forward off the step.

'That ground is 2 miles away Ken, better do something. Arch maybe?'

The wind was incredible, noisy and pushing into his face. He felt the speed pick up and then a slight, very slight, jerking feeling as they stopped accelerating. He felt Art tapping his shoulder, two taps meant... what? Automatically his arms went out to the side, out like wings, that was it, arms out. He had actually done something that he had been trained to do. He was looking at the ground, he had been told not to do that, then he felt Art's hand gently pull his head back again and the camera on Art's wrist appeared in front of his face. Ken looked at the camera and grinned, well he thought that he grinned, in reality the wind was forcing the corners of his mouth up.

Then, somehow, she was there.

Plaid flew up to him, to them, let's not forget about Art, and took his hand, they were hanging in the air, no they were falling through the air, at about 120 mph and his girl, this strange exotic girl in pink and tartan, with a helmet that had cat's ears attached, was holding his hand and smiling. She edged forward. How could she do that when they were going down, were they going down? Ken looked down and felt Arts hand pull his head back, she was still there. How? How was she still there?

Then she kissed him. At 120 mph, she had moved forward, kissed his lips and then backed away. Now they were turning, 360 degrees in a circle, they turned clockwise, until they were facing Plaid again, she was still smiling and blew him another kiss as he saw Art's arms wave above their head. He saw Plaid nod, and the the crazy girl turned 180 degrees, her arms moved behind her and she shot across the sky. Where was she going in such a hurry.

'Maybe the kiss wasn't passionate enough?'

Then they slowed down really quickly, he felt himself jerking on the front of Art, his legs flew out in front of him as they decelerated, ah... his new best friend Art. Now they were moving really slowly, comparatively slowly, it was hard to tell, but they were moving forward too. How was that possible?

He felt Art fussing with things behind him, as he pulled at two yellow toggles they dipped to the left and then the right.

"How was that Ken? Oh we have a good parachute by the way, maybe I should have mentioned that first. I'm just going to loosen up the side straps, just like we discussed on the ground."

'He's lying, he never mentioned that, is it safe to do that, why loosen them?'

He felt a slight drop, maybe an inch, then he felt Art ease the leg straps under the top of his thigh, just a couple of inches.

"More comfortable?" Ken asked.

"Surprisingly yes," Ken answered.

"It's almost like I know what I'm doing eh? Let's look around," and Art turned the parachute to the left and started describing various land features, as they circled. Ken feigned interest, while feeling seriously impressed with how graceful it felt moving around up here.

He stopped the turn and pointed with his right hand to a spot below and in front of them, "There's your girl, down there." What a surprise, a tiny looking pink parachute about 2000 feet below them.

"If you're pointing, who's steering?" Ken asked.

"Oh, I put it on auto-pilot," Art answered.

"Really?"

"No, of course not, don't be daft." Art said with a chuckle.

'Oh, you're a funny man aren't you?"

He pointed to a spot below Plaid and said, "See that huge patch of grass over there? That's where we'll be landing. So, let's talk about the landing. I need you to do two things, and only two things. One, do NOT look at the ground as we come in to land, look at the horizon. Two, when I say 'feet up!' get your legs and feet up to waist level and keep them there until you feel your bum on the ground, got it?"

"Eyes front, feet and legs up, got it," Ken replied.

"Show me," Art said, and Ken did.

"Just do that when I ask. I'm going to fly around until we get to about 1000 feet then I'll set us up to land. Okay?"

Ken was feeling much more relaxed. He looked around at the scenery, the large lake, the city in the distance, and the landing area, approaching more and more rapidly.

"Look, Plaid's landing," Art pointed to the green area. "If she can do it, so can we."

"Reassuring," Ken said. "However, there's a lot that girl can do, that I can't."

"I'm setting us up for landing," Art said. "We're going down wind a little, then I'll turn left and left again. Before you know it we'll be on the ground."

Safely?" Ken asked.

"Hopefully," Art replied. "Now in a few seconds I want you to hold your chest strap with both hands, and look at the horizon. Then, when I say 'Feet Up' get your legs out in front of you."

That's three things, he said two, and two only. You trust this man?'

"No choice at this point," Ken said out loud.

"What's that?" Art asked.

"Sorry inside voice came outside for a moment."

"That's okay, grab that chest strap, look at the horizon, and.... ready, wait for it, FEET UP!" Art yelled loudly.

Ken's legs came up and stayed up as they slid into a sit down landing. The parachute came down behind them and before Ken even realized what was happening, he was unhooked and Plaid had her hand out to help him stand.

Once he was up she grabbed him and planted a hard kiss on his lips before helping him out of his harness. "You did great DI Ken. Aren't mid-air kisses the best, but I like these as well," and she kissed him again. "Next weekend, want to come rock climbing with me?"

Peter Draper © 2025

AIRPORTS, ALIENS, AND TIME WARPS

---∞---

I enjoy going to the airport about as much as having my lips glued to a lamp post.

If I did not arrive at the terminal in time to pick up my dad, I would never hear the end to it.

With foresight, but less common sense, I set the alarm for 4:00 a.m. When I woke up at 4:30 a.m., I was really pissed. This meant I wouldn't have time for breakfast, bathing, shaving, deodorant, or clean underwear, which didn't matter since I was meeting my father…not dating him.

Off I sped to the Dulles Airport, in Washington, DC, to meet me ole pappy. In my overzealous haste to avoid the horrendous early morning traffic jams renowned in Washington, I allowed more than ample time to get there. However, I had not correctly calculated that there would not be any traffic that early on a Saturday morning. This would also explain why I worked as an accountant for the government.

Now I'm at the airport, and I must find a way to kill three hours before the plane arrives. I bought a newspaper with the headline, 'Alien Baby Found On Mars.' Wait a minute, how stupid do they think I am? If we went to Mars *and* found a baby *on* Mars, then it wouldn't be an alien baby but a native baby of Mars...right? Unless it were a human baby from Earth, which would make it an alien baby to the Martians but not to the astronauts since they would be human, too. All I know is that when it comes to little children, if you take your eyes off them for one instant—there is no telling where they will end up.

I was going up on the escalator, standing on the 'right' side. I noticed everyone else was standing on the left. Some woman behind me, wanting to get by, was expecting me to move to the left. The left? Where did she think we were, Beijing? Since when, in America, do we ride, walk, drive, stand, or even loiter on the left? Was I absent the day it was all changed to the left side? Should I look for that 'email,' in my 'junk' folder?

Well, I'll have you know I wasn't going to stand for that, on the left...one *'Yankee Doodle Moment.'* As an American, I know my rights...the right...to stand on the 'right,' the side of right, right as the right does, for right is might. In fact, if it weren't for the Wright Brothers, we wouldn't even be at the airport. I was mad as all heck, and I wasn't going to take it anymore. I took my stand—on the right.

I started studying everyone around me more carefully. They reminded me of how people looked in the classic movie, *'The Invasion of the Body Snatchers.'* Standing there with their empty-headed, dull, vacant stares, looking like a bunch of zombies, albeit well-dressed zombies.

Do you know what I hate about aliens from outer space? They think just because they can build a spaceship and travel a billion light years to another planet, it makes them superior. They always act so smug and arrogant. However, they give themselves away with something as simple as not realizing they are standing on the wrong side of the escalator. Superior beings, my butt, they weren't fooling me.

Due to my government training, I logically figured these aliens were setting up colonies in people's colons, like '*Alien*' (only the other end). Who knew aliens had a sinister plot with all that anal probing. I had always *ass*umed it was just a pleasurable pastime while here on Earth, like in the movie, '*Deliverance*.' Aliens or Hillbillies, it makes no difference when your colon is being colonized.

Looking upon my fellow escalator'ins, I thought: *Aliens are hiding in your butts, you simple-minded humans, forcing you to carry out their diabolical plans, which includes standing on the wrong side of the escalator!* Unfortunately, I must have yelled that out loud, judging by everyone's reaction. It was a good thing this was Washington, DC; everyone here is used to people shouting stupid, bizarre, nonsensical gibberish. We call these people 'politicians' and do our best to ignore them.

On the terminal's upper level, I started following the crowd, walking past all the ticket counters, which were still closed. I hoped there would be some shops or places to get something to eat as I waited for my dad's plane.

Looking for nourishment, I approached a sleepy lady behind the counter of an information booth. "Excuse me, but I woke up late and didn't have time to shower, shave, or put on clean underwear. I was afraid the traffic here in Washington would be so heavy this this time of the morning that I would be delayed arriving here in time to meet my dad, who would have had a hissy fit if he had to wait even a second. He's bad enough when he's in a good mood, though that has been so long I don't remember what that was like. However, I miscalculated, and there really weren't many cars on the road, so I arrived here long before my dad's plane is to arrive and that has left me wondering where I can find something to eat. Can you help me?"

The weary woman muttered, "We only provide information; you will have to go somewhere else for psychiatric counseling…SECURITY."

Eventually, I found a coffee stand right next to the baggage carousel. I purchased a cup of coffee and an apple donut fritter as big as a catcher's glove. I settled in the back of some alcove in the dark, among the extra food and cleaning supplies, to sip my coffee and munch my fritter until the plane arrived.

There were more security and janitorial personnel than travelers. As I sat there, it was all I could do to keep from falling asleep. That would not be good because I was tucked away in the back of a place where they kept unneeded supplies like hotdog buns. Judging from the looks of them, it could be months before they discovered my bloated rotting body if I were to expire like that bakery.

Some guy wearing a janitor's uniform, who *had* been mopping the floor, also seemed to like the seclusion of this little hideaway because he began reclining on the seats opposite of me and was having a restful nap until another guy in a jacket and tie found him. I was out of earshot, but that is when I realized body language can be pretty expressive. The guy in the black windbreaker jacket, who could have been from the same ethnic persuasion as the other one, was standing in front of the younger guy, who was now sitting up. The jacketed one had his arms spread out from his side with palms facing up as if to say, 'Hey Mon, what de hell are you doing? U'r supposed to be cleaning de floor Mon.'

The janitor fellow, busted for napping on the job, assumed a bewildered look on his face, shrugged his shoulders, and loudly explained. "I can't explains it Boss, one moment I be cleaning de floor like I always am doing, Mon, den da next ting u know ah was heer in dis chair an I didn't know dat…till u was yelling at me Mon. It must be sum kind of extraterrestrial parallel co-existent transmutable transmogrification transcendental vortex…or sum sheet like dat…yeah Mon."

The jacketed guy, obviously not convinced, launched into what looked from my vantage point like a long, protracted impromptu employee evaluation—otherwise known as an "ass-chewing.' "I dunno wat 'de hell is wrong with you, Mon. If you weren't my girlfriend's brudder, I would be firing your lazy behind, yeah Mon."

"What do you mean, Boss, I am always doing me job Mon."

"Reely? 'Twas just last week u suppose to be emptying trash cans at 'de loading dock when I found u lying down underneath 'de ticket counter at Pan Am, Mon. U tell me dat you are secret agent for 'de Homeland Security…an u doing surveillance."

"Yeah Boss, an you don't know if dat ain't true," the young janitor said.

"Den Monday, I send you over to 'de warehouse to get cleaning supplies and I don't see you for two days Mon. U tell me you fell into a time-shift paradox an was really here but just moving faster din 'de speed of light. Dat's why I can't see u mopping 'de floor Mon."

"Yeah, dat's right Mon, I was mopping my behind off…yeah Mon."

"En now u tell me u get caught in some parallel vortex. What's next Mon, are u going to be abducted by aliens so dey can do anal probes in yer rectum, Mon?" "Next Tuesday, yeah Mon, I put in 'de vacation slip for dat already, remember…Mon?"

Marley, the Boss said "U come wit me Ziggy, I'm going to have u mop 'de men's room where dare are no parallel universes or swirling vortexes or any aliens flying out 'ur butt Mon." The two of them left with the janitor guy asking the jacketed guy if he's still going to get next Tuesday off because he didn't want to miss a good alien probing if he could help it.

Now I was by myself again, waiting for the plane, which was still an hour away. Alone with just my thoughts. What were my thoughts? Besides planning to have my anus checked for aliens: *If I eat one more bite of this fritter, I'm going to puke.* My dad finally arrived…which is another story all together…yeah Mon.

M. David Lutz © 2025

WHISPERS IN THE WIND

---∞---

I. The Origin

From the breath of the mountains, silent and still,

The wind is born in the twilight chill,

A whisper, a murmur, a gentle sigh,

A spirit of air that kisses the sky.

It dances through valleys and rises to peaks,

Caressing the world with the softness it seeks,

A wanderer eternal, without a home,

The wind is a poet that yearns to roam.

II. The Morning Zephyr

In the dawning light, a zephyr stirs,

Awakening leaves in the slumbering firs,

It glides through the meadows, tender and true,

A messenger clear in the morning dew.

The grasses awaken, the flowers take flight,

As the wind whispers secrets to the growing light,

It teases the petals of roses in bloom,

And scatters their fragrance through the room.

III. The Wind's Song

Listen, oh listen, to the song of the breeze,
It plays on the branches, a melody that frees,
It hums through the hollows and laughs through the leaves,
A hymn to the life that it gently weaves.
The wind is a minstrel with a voice so clear,
It tells ancient tales that all can hear,
Of lovers and battles, of joy and of woe,
Of the cycles of time, of ebb and of flow.

IV. The Tempest

But there are times when the wind is wild,
A tempest, a fury, no longer mild,
It gathers its strength from the ocean's deep,
A roaring force that refuses to sleep.
It lashes the trees with a furious howl,
It topples the mighty and makes giants cowl,
It crashes the waves against the shore,
A relentless hammer, an endless roar.

V. The Desert Wind

Across the sands of the barren plain,
The wind moves softly, again and again,
A phantom that sweeps the dunes with grace,
Leaving no mark, not a single trace.
It carries the whispers of ancient lands,
Of forgotten empires and sunken sands,
The tales of the past in each grain it lifts,
The silent guardian of the desert's gifts.

VI. The Wind's Touch

The wind is a lover with a gentle hand,
It caresses the earth, the sea, and the land,
It lifts up the fallen, it cools the brow,
It offers its solace in the here and now.
A comfort in summer, a chill in the fall,
The wind is a gift that touches us all,
Invisible fingers that brush through the air,
Reminding us always that it is there.

VII. The Storm's Lullaby

In the heart of the storm, there is a calm,

A lullaby sung with a soothing balm,

The wind wraps the world in a soft embrace,

A moment of peace in a chaotic space.

It whispers of hope in the darkest night,

A promise that dawn will bring new light,

The storm will pass, the winds will change,

And life will return to its endless range.

VIII. The Winter Gale

When winter descends with its icy breath,

The wind becomes a herald of death,

It howls through the night with a ghostly moan,

A chilling reminder of the world unknown.

It gathers the snow in swirling flurries,

It blinds the eyes, it hurries, hurries,

A force untamed, a cold so deep,

That even the strongest wish to sleep.

IX. The Wind's Wisdom

The wind carries wisdom from years gone by,
It knows the secrets of earth and sky,
It whispers to those who stop and hear,
The truths that lie both far and near.
It speaks of the past and of things unseen,
Of the spaces between what has been,
It tells of the future in cryptic rhymes,
A sage that exists beyond the times.

X. The Evening's Breeze

As the day retires and the night awakes,
The wind becomes a breath that softly breaks,
It cools the heat of the setting sun,
And tells the stars the day is done.
It sighs through the branches with a gentle ease,
A soothing balm, a tender breeze,
It rocks the world in a cradle of air,
A lullaby sung to everywhere.

XI. The Traveler

The wind is a traveler, forever free,
It journeys across land, sky, and sea,
It knows no borders, it heeds no walls,
It listens to no master, it answers no calls.
It passes through cities with a fleeting grace,
It touches each life, each time, each place,
A silent witness to all that's been,
The wind is a spirit that's always seen.

XII. The Wind's Reflection

And in the stillness, when all is quiet,
The wind reflects on its eternal riot,
It knows it brings both joy and pain,
A paradox that falls like rain.
It is both friend and foe in its flight,
A constant force in the day and night,
A presence that lingers, a voice that sings,
The wind is the soul of all living things.

XIII. The Farewell

When the day is done and the night is deep,
The wind lays down in a gentle sleep,
It whispers a farewell to the moon's soft light,
And promises to return by morning's bright.
It fades into dreams with a silent grace,
Leaving no mark, not a single trace,
But though it may vanish from sight and sound,
The wind's presence is always around.

XIV. The Eternal Dance

For the wind is a dancer that never tires,
It lives in the earth, the air, the fires,
It moves with the stars, it sings with the sea,
An endless dance, wild and free.
It is the breath of life, the voice of space,
A universal song, a timeless grace,
It speaks of the infinite, the vast unseen,
The wind is a bridge to the great serene.

XV. The Wind's Promise

So when you feel the breeze on your face,

Know that the wind is a gift, a grace,

It carries the past, the future, the now,

It speaks to the heart, though we know not how.

For the wind is a friend, a guide, a muse,

A force that we cannot refuse,

It is the spirit that sets us free,

The wind is the breath of eternity.

Damain Nakare II © 2025

THE DREAMSCAPER'S HARVEST

It was just a dream.

Yet, as I sat up peering around my room the sweat pouring down my brow and the steady thumpity, thump, thump, thump!

If you have ever heard the drowning sound of your pulse pounding in your areas only amplified by the bewildering of your heart beating wildly against your ribs - that was the condition of my present state. My eyes frantic and fearful from what I'd dreamed - wandered aimlessly, raking in every crook, every cranny, and every formulated shadow that existed in the space.

Four walls - a box that held me trapped amid pitch black save for the flickering reflection of the tiny nightlight I left on nightly. There was a strange, and sudden prickling that arose upon the nape of my neck.

A chilling feeling that I couldn't shake though I tried - and the creeping drip of my sweat slowly dripped into my eye blinding me from the salt nearly instantly.

Reaching for my phone, I shook my head and attempted to blow it off.

Whoosh!

A sudden rush of air blew over my hand and the phone fell to the floor with a loud thud. I groaned and stood slowly, weakly, from my bed, squinting at the floor only to feel that sudden rush of air now steadily flowing against the nape of my neck. A sound not unlike bones cracking began to snap behind me, and I felt myself instant upturned as a coiling appendage swept me off my feet. I screeched - only to find my mouth suddenly invaded by a coiling and inky whip-like tail with a forked end that hooked into my throat and left me dangling and gagged while I began to drool - spittle and blood suddenly mixing to pour down over my chin and bathe my throat in the thick, sticky fluid. A raspy breath hit my ears and unable to move as I was bound, I whirled around in the air only to come face to face - my eyes wide as quarters and white as the starkest walls as they fell upon my captor.

The reality of what I had run from in the dark recesses of my greying nightmare now had me in a wretched position, writhing as I slowly began to suffocate, and the stench of putridity hit my nostrils causing me to feel both nauseous and light-headed.

The creature, a thing I could not identify as anything other than a cryptid had fangs as long as my forearms, and the saliva that dripped from the being's teeth dripped with the odor of sulfur. Just like one might imagine the scent of fire and brimstone.

Putrefying and intense, the creature stared back at me with deep-set eyes – a dark crimson, near-inky pigment that filled the entirety of its eye sockets and stared back at me with an empty, grimacing almost smirk-like expression. I felt a sudden wetness flick outward at me, sure that I had been spat upon, and squinting my eyes closed the next thing that drew over me was a slimy, slithering appendage and I grunted, feeling my Adam's apple press into the tightening appendage around my throat and mouth and to my horror I realized it was the serpentine creature's tongue!

My hips began to wiggle, as I attempted anything to move away from the disgusting-smelling tongue, but it was useless. My body simply twirled around like a lopsided Piñata having been beaten half to death. If I hadn't already been scared, I was now experiencing sheer terror with palpable and stifling certainty.

The creature's tongue slithered continually across my face - a wet and sickening feeling washing over me with every flicking trace. It was as if it was savoring the taste of my skin - and with every motion, I could feel my heartbeat intensify such that I now wondered if it might explode. A welcome escape from the dreadful and antagonizing fear that now held me in the wrenching grasp of the entity.

Panic had me now so paralyzed that my former movements completely ceased, yet my eyes still felt as if they had been peeled back against my eyelids - nearly popping from my skull.

And still, the coiling appendage that had first gagged me seemed to tighten expelling whatever remaining bits of air that had ballooned within my lungs. Another wave of nauseating breath from the entity hit me in the face then and then with a sudden lurch I watched in horror as the creature's jaws began to separate - further revealing those needle-sharp fangs that now seemed to be as close to my face as my nose and I could feel the pricking pinpoints of one as it slowly scraped against my flesh.

I suddenly blinked my eyes closed and prepared for what I knew would be the inevitable and it was then that everything faded into black.

My ears, prickled at the sounds of crunching bones and in my mind, I knew the creature's jaws had separated even more – my suspicion solidified when the tearing of my skin suddenly broke through the muscle, and I heard a new snapping sound. The eerie sound of my skull splitting, and I knew the entity had bitten into my head now, but I had no way to fight it off.

"Am I going to die?"

I wondered, then hoping that the pain I was feeling as my brain was penetrated at last by the creature's canines, I felt a sudden sensation of euphoria.

Crunch – the sound of my skull collapsing was all that I could hear now though my pulse had accompanied it like a low drumming accompaniment to the main acoustics that banged in my eardrums. On either side, I felt as if my entire head was now inside the beast's maw and any hope I'd had of an escapade from my nightmare upon waking instantly faded – as did my consciousness and the creature consumed the essence of me in one chomping bite.

The End.

Sai Marie Johnson © 2025

THE STRANGER

———∞———

'Have you seen that new feller who's moved into Barbara Green's cottage?'

Julia Ashley was addressing a comment to her friend Alison Winter as they queued one Friday morning in the post office of their small Cornish village.

'No. Why?'

'Well, they say he's rather odd.'

'How do you mean?'

'According to Fred Allsop, he's quite surly,' explained Julia, 'or at least he doesn't say much. He went into Fred's shop to buy some tools and Fred said it was like talking to a robot. You know what Fred's like. He's very chatty but he couldn't get a thing out of him. He's quite good looking though.'

'How do you know that? Have you seen him?'

'Yes, I was passing by Barbara's old place and he was just putting his key in the door. I should say he's in his late thirties, maybe forty. He looks a bit like Sean Connery but without the cheeky smile – well, as Connery used to look in those James Bond films.'

'He's too young for us then, Dear,' replied Alison with a chuckle, 'but he might set a few young hearts fluttering. There aren't too many Sean Connery look-a-likes round here. What's he called, this young chap?'

'I haven't a clue.'

'At least not yet,' laughed Alison, 'but I bet it won't be long till you find out. Not much passes you by Julia Ashley.'

****

On Saturday morning the stranger was looking round Jim Brown's boatyard and showing particular interest in a Monterey 256 Cruiser.

'Nice little boat that, Sir,' said Jim, anxious to make a sale.

'Not bad, but needs a bit of work doing. How much is it?'

'Well, let me see now, I could let you have it for £15,000.'

'No doubt, but it's more than I want to pay, particularly with the work it needs.'

They quickly settled on £13,000.

'Would you deliver it to the harbour here, please.'

'Certainly, I'll do it on Monday if that's all right with you. Incidentally have you got a berth there?'

'Yes, I have.'

'Planning on doing a little fishing?'

'Yes, and scuba diving.'

'Take my advice, Sir, and be careful. There's a very strong current out there, particularly just off the headland.'

'I'll remember that.'

The deal was finalised in the office and Jim Brown was left scratching his head, having just completed his quickest sale he'd ever done to the most taciturn buyer he'd ever had.

****

The stranger had moved into Barbara Green's old cottage only one week previously and yet his reputation was already spreading throughout the village. The cottage was on the harbour front and it was here that he was now regularly setting up his easel to paint the harbour and its activities. People stopped to look at his work and tried to strike up a conversation but in return got only monosyllabic responses.

On Sunday morning he went to church and afterwards was persuaded by the Reverend Tim Blake to stay for a coffee with a few of the regulars. He reluctantly did so but was almost as withdrawn as before. He declined an invitation from Letitia West to join the local art club and another from Brian Westlake to consider joining the scouting movement, although surprisingly he did agree to run a session on survival outdoors at some time in the future. At least the vicar elicited that the stranger's name was John Kent. He also opined to his wife that John Kent's hands seemed to shake when he drank coffee. He sensed there was a nervous tension about him.

Of course, rumours circulated about John Kent, mostly around a common theme that he had a disreputable past and that he'd come to the village to start a new life. However, even if he was reforming, it would be wise to keep children away from him. His reputation was not enhanced one day after he'd positioned himself outside the local supermarket with a chair and a table, stickers and badges, and a collecting box for the Royal British Legion.

Onlookers said that a young man had told him there was no longer any need for the Armed Forces and that he should clear off. War mongering was not welcome. Whilst the onlookers favoured John Kent's charitable drive, his reaction was thought to be unacceptable. Apparently he'd grabbed the young man by the collar and whispered something into his ear. The man had left with a look of abject fear on his face. He was not from the village and had not been seen since.

Matters came to a head on the day of the village fete. The fete itself was a jolly event with a good turnout, a wide range of stalls, plenty of colourful bunting and music by a local band. John Kent took a walk around, bought a couple of books and went into the beer tent to buy a half a pint of real ale. Ahead of him in the queue were two young, rough looking men at the counter and John noticed one of them hand over a £10 note for two pints. When the girl served him she gave him the change but he complained he'd given her £20 and a disagreement broke out. Eventually John intervened.

'I'm sure you've made a genuine mistake,' he said, 'but I saw you give the young lady £10.'

'Mind your own bloody business,' was the response from the larger and the fatter of the two.

John suggested to the girl that she should not give him change for £20 and that if the troublemaker wanted to make a formal complaint, he would support the girl.

'You're the troublemaker mate,' replied the thug, 'and if you don't back off you'll regret it,' at the same time putting his hand around John's throat.

What happened next was so fast it was almost a blur but John appeared to put his right hand behind the thug's left ear. In fact, John had pressed a knuckle into the hollow behind his ear, putting considerable pressure on the parotid lymph node. The effect was that the thug squealed in pain, let go of his hold on John and doubled up clutching his head.

'What have you done to 'im?' shouted the smaller thug, surprised but not anxious to get physically involved.

'Oh, don't worry. He'll be all right before very long. I suggest you take him home.'

'You'll pay for this,' groaned the large one, still clutching his head and being led out by his friend.

****

In the evening of the same day, John was quietly drinking a pint of local real ale in the Royal Oak when the two local roughs came in and made a point of staring at him as they made their way to the bar. It was clear that they'd been drinking quite heavily during the afternoon and were now ready for an evening session.

John ignored them and got on with his Telegraph crossword. As he was within walking distance of his house in the harbour, he decided to have a second pint, which would hopefully give him time to solve the remaining four clues. It did and he was able to put away his pen with some satisfaction before leaving to walk home. He was not aware that the two roughs were hot on his heels.

George Harper, the owner, was surprised but pleased to see the two louts, Fred and Bill Gundry, leave so early. They were a couple of local farmworkers who frequently drank too much and made a nuisance of themselves. This promised to be a quiet evening with them out of the way. He did hear some shouting outside but paid no attention since youths were not unknown to make a noise walking about in groups.

Five minutes later, John Kent came back into the bar and suggested to George that he should call an ambulance.

There'd been a little trouble outside and the Gundry brothers needed medical attention. He himself had a cut on his face but otherwise seemed all right.

****

The story was soon passed round the village, giving rise to two principal viewpoints. In the minority were those who saw the episode as a further example of the malpractice of the suspicious newcomer. Most saw it as just retribution for the long- running loutish behaviour of the Gundry brothers. However, none was as incensed as the father of the brothers, Mr Bert Gundry, who decided to take the matter to court, citing grievous bodily harm as the charge against John Kent.

John decided to find a solicitor to represent him in the magistrates' court and was recommended by George Harper to see a Miss Penelope James in the local town. George had been impressed by John's action against the brothers who'd been a constant problem for him.

Penelope, in her late thirties, was a divorcee who'd had a very difficult first marriage. When John first met her in her office, she was dressed in a smart mid-blue suit which set off her strawberry blond hair. She had pale blue eyes that stared fixedly at him when he spoke as though challenging him not to deviate one iota from the truth, and a no-nonsense manner that obliged him to think carefully before speaking. John quickly came to the conclusion that he was glad she was on his side.

As it happened, she had an assistant who lived in John's village. Consequently, when John had finished giving his account of the incident outside the Royal Oak, she was already forearmed in asking about his relationships with others in the village. His rather non-committal reply prompted her to summarise the position at that point.

'On the whole, we have a good case. You were acting in good faith, and the Gundry brothers are known to be troublemakers. Unfortunately, you, too, have acquired a less than sympathetic reputation among some people in the village which, as things stand, will not act in your favour. I need to ask you some personal background questions.'

Initially John was reluctant to provide details but, as Penelope pointed out, there were no witnesses to the fight and if the magistrate saw fit, he or she could remand the case to the crown court with a charge of grievous bodily harm and a heavy penalty if he was found guilty.

With that, John recounted his career as a captain in the Strategic Air Service and his service in Iraq before and during the war against Saddam Hussein. He was captured, tortured but survived. Later he served in Afghanistan, where he also had a difficult experience.

When he'd finished, Penelope paused and then said,

'I need your agreement for you to have a medical examination'.

'There's no need,' sighed John. 'I've had plenty of examinations by a variety of specialists, including psychiatrists and psychologists. I have PTSD: post-traumatic stress disorder.'

'Which can cause you to lose your temper very easily?'

'It can, although I've learned to walk away if there's a problem. Outside the pub I couldn't walk away. I was attacked.'

****

In the magistrate's court, John was exonerated and the Gundry brothers were found guilty of common assault, fined and ordered to do community service. To celebrate and to show his appreciation, John invited Penelope to dinner. Normally she kept her private and professional lives separate but she made an exception on this occasion, and this marked the start of an ongoing friendship. The case was widely publicised in the area and, as his background became known, John was accepted warmly into the community. The Grundy brothers on the other hand felt obliged to maintain a low profile and they certainly sought to avoid another run-in with John Kent.

Michael W. Brookes © 2025

THE RAVEN

Oh, don't mind me, I am just passing through.

You need not worry about my small frame or if I am going to disturb you.

What is this? Prose beneath you nose?

Do you mind if I have a look at it? I want to see how this goes.

A tree, a few side characters and no mystery. Really?

How can you put this down without any foresight or clarity?!

You need to try harder! Scrap it and start again!

Don't waste a word if it doesn't deserve to play a part in the tale my friend.

Ok, this looks a bit better, but what are they supposed to do when they reach the bridge?

Cast a spell? Please try to be original, that trope has been done to the death and is only popular among kids.

Use the creativity you have and stretch the truth a bit more.

Collate a collection of crafty solutions that nobody has ever seen before.

This is now starting to look like a novel.

Don't stop now, you are on a roll, no time to dawdle.

That's it! Ignore the cramp in your hand and your back as you write.

You will have a story worth telling by the end of tonight.

The candle has been snuffed out.

It seems it is time for me to depart, there is no more work to be done here no doubt.

No need to thank me, just trust yourself a little more than you care to know.

My name? Oh, you can call me "Poe".

The Paper Man © 2023

UNCONSCIOUS WRITINGS

---∞---

I'm going to tell you a story that you will remember every night when you go to sleep.

A few years ago, on an ordinary night, something happened that changed my life forever. Just remembering it makes my body shiver and my ears ring.

It was a warm spring night. It wasn't hot enough to turn on the fan, so once I got ready for bed, I just turned off the light and went to bed. The room was completely silent, and no noise could be heard from the street.

I couldn't sleep. I was strangely restless. I turned sideways on my right arm and got tangled in the sheet. I started feeling relaxed, but something didn't feel normal. The room was quieter and darker than usual. Not even a little light came through the window. But I got really tired, and I closed my eyes for the last time.

'-*Fuuuuu*-'

I got goosebumps, and my pulse quickened. I covered my head with the sheet. I felt like someone had blown on my left ear, but I was alone. Something in me had changed. I had the feeling of wanting to take away something I had inside. I needed to turn on the light, but I was afraid to come out of my hiding place. I stuck out my arm and felt around until I found the switch for the nightstand. I took courage and suddenly uncovered myself; there was nothing and no one. It hadn't been my imagination. Someone had been there. I could even sense its closeness. But who? And why? I had not believed in spirits or paranormal things until that moment.

That night, I didn't sleep. I couldn't. I relived that feeling for hours, trying to understand, trying to find a rational explanation. I couldn't either. Every time sleep overcame me, I would wake up hearing whispers in my mind.

The following night, I was terrified. I was afraid to go to bed, and the same thing would happen. But I was too tired.

I went to bed. This time, I even put a blanket over the sheet. I wanted to feel safe, covered by something thicker. I covered myself from head to toes, leaving just enough space to breathe, and took my arm out of the cocoon I had formed to turn off the light on the nightstand. I waited to see if I had heard anything. I was tense and I think any little sound would have made me jump out of bed. Nothing happened. I couldn't resist anymore and surrendered to sleep.

The next morning, the sun coming through the window woke me up. The cocoon had fallen apart. I slept better than ever. I yawned, stretched, and just then I touched something under the sheet. When I picked it up, I was stunned.

There was a black pen and several sheets of paper lying on the mattress cover, which was all scratched with black ink. What had happened? The last thing I remembered was falling asleep.

I grabbed all the pages and tried to find an order. I saw my handwriting, but it was impossible for me to have written that. The text was clear and neat. I started reading with the feeling of reading something foreign.

"Daniela was thirty years old and had a career with a great future. She didn't know that everything was about to change. Life would give her a big surprise."

Seeing my own name on the sheet worried me greatly. When reading, I experienced a sensation of a double voice within my mind. Mine and that of a man with a deep, hoarse voice.

"As the days passed, she found hints that caught her attention. But on the last day, she defined her future.

Life can be as short or as long as one wishes. You have to know how to listen and make decisions, and Daniela learned how to do it the hard way."

I felt goosebumps from head to toes.

"The morning of the third day was decisive. She woke up early and felt the need to miss work and stay home. As the hours passed, she began to feel bad, very bad. Her chest hurt, her ears were ringing and everything was spinning around her. She managed to lie down on the couch, but felt her soul leave her body.

She began to beg. She begged for her life, even though there was no one to hear her. Or so she thought.

"I promise to do anything you ask. I want to live." She said in a low voice. She didn't know who she was talking to but had the instinct to seal a pact with a higher power. She felt footsteps around her that were moving away. The trembling of her body stopped, and her heart rate returned to normal.

Without knowing it, days later she had to fulfill what she promised. She felt weak; she was emaciated and her mood was no longer the same. When she left home, she found a note on the window of her car.

"Today, someone will have to suffer if you want to smile again".

She was confused, but she had already experienced that there was a higher power that could change her life. With regret, she thought a lot about that request. At the end of the day, she hadn't done anything; Her morals prevented it, but the discomfort appeared and was getting worse.

Coming back from work, she couldn't take it anymore and did the first thing that came to mind. She closed her eyes, held on to the wheel, and ran a red light. Her negligence caused a tremendous shock. She accelerated. She wanted to escape. A few blocks later she regained her strength, her breath, and began to smile. She felt powerful. She arrived at her house in a state of total ecstasy. Something she had never felt like before. She soon understood how everything worked.

What was I reading? The double voice in my mind felt almost like a memory.

"Finally, the long-awaited last day had arrived without her noticing. It was a splendid afternoon, and she was stronger and more confident than ever. That day, she had not found any notes. She thought it was all over.

When night came, she went to dinner at her grandmother Norma's house. Everything was going on normally until, while washing the dishes, under one of them, she found what she had been unconsciously waiting for all day. The note said:

"You will disappear your roots to flourish".

She understood it almost instantly and almost knocked the dishes on the floor. Although her life was at stake, she did not believe she could fulfill this request. Just weighing the possibility of it distressed her.

She wielded a knife with all her might, returned to the dining room and found her grandmother asleep in the chair. She knew her life would end. She was not going to be able to comply with such an insane request. She kissed her on the forehead and hurried back to her house.

The cards had been laid out. There was nothing more to do and Daniela knew what the end would be like."

I was absorbed in reading. Thousands of questions were rushing through my mind. There was no way I could have written all that and not remember it. But I couldn't find a rational explanation.

Had I gone crazy?

At the end of the day, I started to feel very bad; I had tachycardia, and I was short of breath. I immediately related it to the story. I tried to calm down and little by little I succeeded. That night, I woke up more than once hearing voices. I was losing my mind and couldn't talk to anyone about it.

A burning sensation throughout my body woke me up in the middle of the morning. When I turned on the light, I saw my arms and legs with scratches, some deeper than others.

I decided not to go to work; I called in sick, and I think I was. But no one could help me. During the day, my condition worsened; dizziness, nausea, loss of consciousness... I couldn't go on like this, and I couldn't stop thinking about the story. I had the terrible idea that perhaps those were the steps to follow.

I staggered into the car and tried to drive to fulfill the plan. I thought I wouldn't be able to, but I did just as I had read, and I didn't know what happened behind me. I went back and locked myself in my room and noticed an absolute improvement within a few hours.

It was at that moment that I knew for sure what was happening. As the days passed, I went into seclusion. I was afraid.

When I got the call from my grandmother, I knew it was my last day. I was afraid to go see her, but I wanted to say goodbye to her. I knew there was no way I could hurt her.

That night, we had dinner, we laughed, and I enjoyed her company like never before. But when midnight arrived, everything changed. Everything began to spin around me and the voices in my head stunned me. I fainted, but when I half recovered, I convinced my grandmother that she just needed to go and rest. I got up to leave, and she looked at me, worried.

I will never forget that night. It was at that moment that I knew what I was and was not capable of doing.

Many years have passed since that moment, but every May 6 I return to her grave to leave her flowers and ask for forgiveness.

Mariela Ivón Armando © 2024

LOVE SERENDIPITY

---∞---

Your beauty is like ripples on the ocean, and your heart is pure with love and devotion.

You love everyone, including your friends, but most of all, you're there till the end.

Even though we are far apart, our minds and our hearts are never apart.

With all things that are and all things that will be, maybe you are the one that true love can be.

If it wasn't you then sad would be true, but under life's ever gaze, things can always be true.

If you try hard enough in the life of love, our world will collide, but we will be by each other's side.

Being with me is not gonna be easy, but if you succeeded, you shall be busy.

I don't give my heart freely, because life has been very harsh, but I'm also very kind and sweet, just like a chocolate marsh.

I'm very moody in several different ways, but you can always guarantee that love will light the way.

I'm very protective of my heart until it's proven true, but at the end of the day, it can only be one person and that person is you.

Curtis L. L. Herbold © 2024

THE CHIN

---∞---

Dedicated to somebody who used to be cool,
a long, long time ago.
A brilliant child (and wealthy, too).
She had so much to lend.

But, deep inside, she held a shame:
she had a double chin.
Skinny girls looked down on her,
and she looked down on them.

High school life is made much worse
when you don't quite fit in.
Time went by, and it still hurt,
those pains of teenage life.

So, she conspired to show them all,
and go under the knife.
Nowadays, she looks quite lean.
You'll always see her grin.

The joke's on us: we're middle-aged,
    and all have double chins!
But, lend your ear a moment more;
    that's not quite where it ends.

For, when she shed her extra chin,
    she also lost a friend.
Her arrogance juts from her face
    more sharply than that chin.

Not only did the outside change,
    but something changed within.
So, nowadays, I leave her be,
    her and her single chin.

She may be looking leaner,
but I liked her more back then.

Peter McCollum © 2024

FUTURES HENCE

∞

I snuggled into the crook of the wall, the bricks catching and pulling the hairs on the back of my neck. With one hand, I cupped my chin, then pushed it up and to the right until I heard and felt a string of *pops*. People always asked me, "With your seniority, why do you still go down?" The dark was cool and comfortable, the breeze blowing in my face quite pleasant. That was one reason why I still came down: the feel of actual wind.

The breeze changed directions and carried the sharp, sour stink of bar's dumpster along with it. I did my best to shut it out, but it was not easy, and it was certainly not welcome. Which came to the other reason why I was one of the few Cappers who would come down anymore: bonus pay to risk the smells or whatever else was in the air. There were no bonuses for the distractions that went along with coming down. As a Capper, distractions could be just as lethal as whatever might be in the air or breeding in a puddle.

A soft voice whispered into my earpiece, "It's coming now. We got it thrown out." I pressed the thumbnail-sized earpiece deeper into my ear, grateful for that much: my target would be coming to me, making my job that much easier. Inside, his message given, my contact would beat it. It never paid to be on the scene when a Capper delivered. I reached under my trench coat to take my snub-nosed 50-caliber Enforcer out of the back of my belt and unbuttoned the top two buttons of my shirt with my free hand so it would be a little less restricting if I needed to be able to move more freely. It would not be long; my job would be done, then I could go home to a hot bath and safe, sanitized air. I cleared my throat, hacked, and spat out phlegm. That was not good. I had been on the street too long already; my antivirals were wearing off or being overpowered, and I was getting sick.

"Shit."

I opened my mouth wide and moved my jaw to no effect, then plugged my nose with thumb and forefinger, clamped my mouth shut and blew, finally managing to unplug my ears. Not good just got worse. Whatever I had caught was already in my ears, which could affect my balance, which could also get me killed.

"Out'a here!" a man's harsh voice came.

I looked over just in time to see a figure tossed out the bar's back door. It was a "her." She fell ungracefully to the asphalt, skinning her chin and hands. The first thing to hit was her chin, so it was no surprise when she did not move immediately. The burly man spat in her direction, the glob of glistening saliva arcing up and then down onto the back of her thigh. I did not like that. I could arrest him for that on a 245, assault with a deadly weapon for exposing her to potentially hazardous waste, but I was not in the mood. When he turned, I glimpsed the wide patch of a scabbed rash on the back of his neck above his collar, one of the signs of long-term use of low-end antivirals. If nothing else, it marked him as normal. He slammed the door behind him, rocking the light mounted to the wall beside the door jam. After a count of ten, she looked back, her eyes narrowed in pain or anger, I really did not care which.

Then again, if I did not care, why was I still waiting? I removed my ear-piece and dropped it into my trench-coat pocket.

"I don't need you anyway," she muttered, but her voice was thick with emotion. She sat up, caught a big drop of blood as it fell off her chin and wiped it on her pants. She had red-orange hair and a pretty enough face — for what she was — but she had a quirk about her. Something was somehow ... off. I twisted my moustache with one hand and thought about it for a moment. It came to me: she was perfectly healthy. She was not rashy, not coughing, not dripping snot, not even weepy eyes. It marked her as clearly as the other's rash marked him. She was not even trying to conceal her genetics. She might have even be using it. There were still ones like her selling their blood, saliva — even sexual fluids! — with the promise of their genetic immunities. It was rare to catch it from them, but there were still cases every once in a while.

She groaned, cradling her hands against her chest. She rocked back and forth on her knees, not stopping as she lifted her hands to blow on the bleeding scrapes as a tear rolled down her cheek.

I returned my Enforcer to the back of my pants and stood. I would not need it to pick this one up — she was not dangerous. "Hey," I said and stepped out of the shadows.

She jerked her head in my direction, startled, then went back to blowing on her hands for about a three-count, then she looked back again, but slowly. I could see the realization dawn as her expression changed: I was just as healthy. She stared at me with wide eyes, the whites showing all the way around. "I — I was just thrown out! I didn't make any money!"

"I don't want money, I've *got* a job," I said coolly, my hair blowing softly on the top of my head, because my scalp was shaved from the tops of my ears down.

"I'm already bleeding," she said. "Lucky you. If you've got a jar ... I'll bleed in it. You can have it. No charge."

"I just want you, Mongo."

"Oh, God ...!" she gasped as her fears were confirmed: she knew exactly what I was. No doubt, someone saying those five words had haunted her nightmares since the Mutation Edict of 2092. Worse, since she did not take advantage of the Mars Asylum Grant of 2126.

"Make it easy on yourself," I said. "Just come along quietly." I waved toward the open end of the alley. She glanced that way and her eyes went grudgingly up to the light-ridden disc of Upper York, a thousand feet up, safely nestled inside an insulation dome. Another tear rolled down her cheek.

"What have I done to *you?*" she whispered as a thick drop of blood ran down the middle of her neck.

"Nothin'. Nothin' at all. Now stop all that whining." I walked over, grabbed her wrist and hoisted her to her feet. "Show some backbone for God's sake!"

She jerked her wrist out of my grasp, and I noticed some of her blood on my fingers. I licked it off: *good luck.* Hope lit in her eyes. "No, really, do you have a jar? I'll even give you my other fluids. I'll give them to you the fun way. I'm clean. We're immune to STDs, too. Immune to *all* disease." I pushed her ahead of me, toward the open end of the alley. I sniffed and she looked back at me sharply. "Your AVs are wearing off. You're getting congested. I mean it: whatever fluids you want. Any *way* you want." Another tear rolled down her cheek. *"Please."*

"Stop talkin'," I said and shoved her around the corner of a building toward my car, a shiny new UDX 5000. First, I did not like interacting with Mongos. Second, she was right. My head was stuffing up more and more every minute. I raised my wrist-piece to my lips and said, "Open passenger door." It lifted, rotating on a forward hinge and she froze, staring at it. "Get in." She did not move, other than her eyes. I saw the shift to look at me sidelong. My adrenaline started to flow as I realized that I was wrong: she was going to attack or to run. Either way, I had misjudged. I reached under my trench coat as she turned and stepped in, caught my face with both hands — and kissed me on the mouth.

Her tongue thrust between my teeth, grinding against mine, and I might have enjoyed it if she was not what she was — and if we were not staring into each other's eyes the whole time. Her eyes were green with little yellow flecks and her eyelashes matched her hair and eyebrows. She broke off the kiss and licked my top lip, then my bottom one before she stepped back. "Extra sloppy," she whispered. "More spit."

I licked my lips and swallowed, then took my hand off my Enforcer, leaving it in the back of my pants. I pointed at my car. She got in and I made to slam the door down, but all I did was start it swinging smoothly closed on its own. I clenched my teeth and took a deep breath to calm down. *What's wrong with me? Why did I let this Mongo do that?* It was not the first time one had offered me her fluids the "fun way" ... I never let any of them kiss me. That is, when they tried, they ended up on the ground, bleeding. I took another breath, let it out. Was my head opening up? I raised my wrist-piece to my lips and said, "Open driver door," then walked around to the other side. I got in even before it finished opening and gave it a tug to start it closing again. She had not moved. Without looking at her, I ordered, "Don't do that again."

"Isn't it helping? It should be clearing up your congestion by now. If not, give it a few minutes —"

"Quiet!"

She hunched in on herself, her hands in her lap, palms up. Most of the scrapes were a darker shade of red, starting to scab over. "Why ... why do want to you do this to — to me?" A sob exploded from her lips an instant before she got herself back under control.

I pressed my foot on the accelerator, activating the electric engine, and pulled away from the curb into the scarcely peopled street, waiting for the green square to light up on my dashboard. In my peripheral, I saw a tear fall onto her fingers.

She reached for me, holding out her hand, index and middle fingertips wet. "Here," she whispered. "You can have it." I licked my lips but resisted the temptation. "Open your mouth, stupid." Normally, I would have smacked her in the teeth for talking to me like that but, again, I did nothing. No, I opened my mouth. She stuck her fingers in and I cleaned off the tear, as well as a little bit of metallic blood. When she put her hand down, I noticed that the green square had lit up and touched it. The UDX lifted off the ground on a magnetic cushion and the rubber tires withdrew into the car's frame. We started to rise at a steep angle, quickly getting steeper, until we were on a vertical.

I glanced at her. "First time in a UDX?" When she did not answer, I grimaced. "In answer to your question: why do I want to do this to you? It's not that I want to or don't want to. It's not personal. It's my job. Mongos are illegal. I'm just servin' my country."

"I'm a *person!*" she cried, loud enough to make me wince. "That makes it personal!" She whirled toward me and, for just a second, I wondered if leaving my Enforcer against my spine was a mistake, then she wilted again and whispered, "I've got rights."

"You're a Mongo," I answered simply. "Nothin' in the Constitution about Mongos."

"I care, I love — I fear!" she argued, voice regaining some strength. "How am I different from you?"

"You're a Mongo," I repeated.

Outside, the roofs of Lower York finally fell away. I took a deep breath through my nose and air flowed freely. It felt like I was in perfect health. The problem was, I had no idea how many dozens of bacterial infections and viruses I had been exposed to while on the street. Any one of them, if allowed to grow, could kill me, even after swallowing her saliva. I touched another button on the dashboard and a gentle breeze filled the cabin: air laced with antibiotics, antivirals and virus-targeting enzymes.

"You don't need that," she said softly. "With me, you won't *ever* need that. Not ever again. I've already given it to you, because I care. See? Proof. I *care*. And I can tell you're different from other Cappers. I can see it. I could love you. I know I could. Take me to Upper York with you. Everyone's healthy there. I won't stand out. You'll just have a new girlfriend. A wife even!"

"You're a Mongo."

"I'd have no choice but to be loyal. To be devoted. You would have my life in your hands. That would guarantee that my love would never falter. Never stray."

"You. Are. A Mongo!"

"Is it my fault I was born?!" she wailed, once again loud enough to narrow my eyes.

"Nope," I answered. "But a Mongo's a Mongo." I shifted into forward mode, pressed the accelerator toward the floor and turned the wheel, my UDX banking smoothly to the left, nudging her toward me. She made no attempt to resist, remaining against my shoulder and upper arm.

"Please tell me your name," she whispered.

I straightened up quickly and pulled away from her, giving the wheel a tug to help get her off my arm as we headed toward the Lower York city limits. "Why the hell would you ask that?"

"Mine's KaeLene."

I glanced at her. "KaeLene. As in KL-33-N."

She blinked and all expression left her face. In fact, her fair skin might have gotten a shade more pale.

"How long have you even been out?" When she did not answer, I did for her. "Not long enough to know to choose a name different from your Batch Code. *Now* who's stupid?"

"See?" she whispered. "You could protect me. You could save me. Isn't that what you do? You uphold the law to *protect* people ... like me."

I pointed at her sharply. "Stop talkin'."

"What would *you* name me?"

"I said stop!"

"Can I have a final request? Name me."

"You gotta be kiddin' me," I muttered, glancing at her. She turned in the seat to face me. The stripe of red down the center of her neck had reached down between her breasts and had turned dark red as it dried. I traced it back up to her face, her red-orange hair, her green eyes, the scabbing scrape on her chin, the light spotting of orange freckles on her nose. She was not "pretty enough" ... she was lovely. I gave my head a shake and looked out the windshield. "There's an Irish goddess with hair like yours. Eyes like yours. Her name was Brid. When baby girls were born in Ireland, many were named Brid, Brigid, or Brigit ... after this goddess." I grimaced. "So I'd name you Brid."

She did not respond and, after a minute or so, I looked back to see that he face was pink and she was crying again. Her body shook as she sobbed quietly. "Thank you," she whispered, although I could barely understand it. "That's so beautiful. I didn't know what a lot of those words meant, but I know they were beautiful."

I hit the steering wheel with the heel of my hand and she yipped, startled. "Why didn't you go to Mars with the rest of the Mongos?!"

"And be a slave?"

"*Not* a slave! You'd work for a megacorp till you repaid your transport! Far more important, Mongos aren't *illegal* on Mars! Seems like a damn good deal to me!"

"Why am I different?" she whispered.

"Be serious," I snapped. "Mutation. That's all the answer you need."

"No. Not that. *Me.*" She paused and grinned. "Brid. Me. Why am I so different? I can tell you're an experienced Capper. You don't get upset like that with every Mongo."

"Lady —"

"Call me Brid. Last request, remember?"

I let out a tight breath. "Fine." I glanced at her sidelong. "Brid, why would you stay when you had the chance to get the hell out of here?"

"Family."

"Why wouldn't they go?"

"They were too old to go to Mars," she answered. "But not too old to be farmed."

I glanced at her again.

"The pharmas like the older ones, I think," she said, a haunted look in her eyes. "They don't fight, or not as hard if they do."

"Did you say 'farmed'?"

She pushed up her sleeve to show me a shunt just below her elbow joint. "That one's for blood. I have others." Her eyes narrowed. "How could you not know that? That's why the Mongos weren't exterminated that couldn't go to Mars. Our fluids are harvested for pharmaceuticals." She waved a finger in the air. "You might be breathing me right now."

I turned it off.

"See? You *are* different." She smiled her triumph. It was like a kick to the gonads. It helped me get my head back together, regain my detachment, my professionalism.

"I'm a Capper," I stated matter-of-factly. "You're a Mongo. You should've gone to Mars. Failin' that, you shouldn't have escaped your host."

"Or maybe I was wrong," she whispered. I could hear the life drain out of her. I had heard it so many times, I recognized it instantly.

"No more talkin'."

"No," she cried, leaning toward me all over again. She grabbed my upper arm with both hands and squeezed. "It wasn't *us* that did it! It was *your* search for immunities and expanded potential and serial immortality and — and — and —" She stopped. I was not listening. I did not even try to get her hands off my arm. She leaned closer. "It was *your* search for extended life. *Your* war against mutated sickness. Is it our fault our immunities couldn't be bred into you?" I did not answer. She let go and sat back in her seat. "Ever think *we're* the future? God works in mysterious ways and — even through the hands of genetic engineers! When humanity suddenly out-selected the Neanderthal, it was a mutation! Why not again? Why not now? Why *wouldn't* God use *your* hands to counteract the new plague? Wouldn't God take action to keep His children alive?"

"I've heard it all before," I stated simply, but it was reflexive. My "not listening" was a sham. For some reason, I could not shut her voice out like I did with the others. I *had* heard it all before. Well, other than the stuff about God. The Neanderthal Argument was the staple of every Mongo's repertoire. My answer was stock: Neanderthals are extinct. So comparing us to the Neanderthal is *not* the right path to choose when trying to persuade.

Lower York passed away below us and I shifted into landing mode. Brid had maintained her silence for the longest time since I had met her. When I looked over, she was staring up through the T-top at Upper York. Even though we had passed beyond the city limits, Upper York still blotted out the stars for another five miles beyond our position. "I've never been out from under Upper York," she said quickly. "Can I change my last request?"

"Nope." The sound of motors turning out the wheels told me we were about to touch down, then the UDX rocked as we did. Altogether, it took about two minutes. The engine powered down automatically, and I said, "Open both doors." They rotated upward. I ordered, "Get out."

"D-do you know what it's like?" she whispered and grabbed my arm again. "H-hated wherever I go ...? *Worse* than meat in some places ...?"

"The sob story of every Mongo." I pulled one of her hands off my arm, then twisted free of the other and got out of the car, sighing my irritation. "Get out."

"You said you'd call me Brid!"

"Get out, Brid."

Voice raw with emotion, she said, "Not until you tell me your name!"

I sighed again, but harder. It was totally unlike me to let one of them get to me like this. I waited for her to climb out of the car, but she did not move. After another minute, I walked around to the other side and pointed at the ground, but still she would not move. "Brid."

"No. Your name."

"Payt. My name's Payt."

She swung her legs out of the car, but remained seated and whispered, "Why won't you listen to me, Payt?"

"Hey," I said, spreading my hands. "It's nothin' against you. I'm just servin' my country. Get out of the car, Brid." I took out my Enforcer and stared down at the dirt for a moment, waiting. "Now."

What was the matter with me? On any other day, I would have jerked her out of the car and stood for none of her blubbering, let along everything else. I looked back at her: she stared up at me with shiny, glowing eyes, still not moving. She was waiting for me to make a decision, I could sense it. At the same time, I did not think that she expected me to let her go … she seemed to understand that her time was near its end. What was she waiting for? What was all that talk about God? What was she trying to do? I ground my teeth. When I looked back, she had lowered her head, then she took my free hand in both of hers ... laid my palm on the crown of her head. Breeze blew red-orange strands of hair between my fingers. She was at my mercy, just as she had always been, but now she acknowledged it openly.

Mercy.

The quality of mercy is not strained ... it droppeth as the gentle rain ... from Heaven to the place beneath ....

No, not from Heaven, from me.

I removed my hand and took two steps back, then gestured with my weapon. "Make a run for it."

She did not react; did not even blink.

"C'mon, I made an offer." I clenched my teeth, looked at the red rivulet running down the center of her throat and splitting her cleavage.

I was breaking the law, violating my vows, and she was not even doing anything about it! It made me angry. What did she want from me? No, I knew the answer to that. She had laid it out pretty clearly: she wanted me to take her back to Upper York with me. I kicked the dirt angrily.

"Run!" I ground my teeth and gestured violently with my Enforcer as I turned my face toward the dark horizon. "I'm not even gonna watch. Go. We never met." When I turned back, she was still there. "Okay, that must have been too easy," I said. "Guess I should'a had you pegged from the start. You're one of those Mongos that gets off churnin' up a Capper's guts. No challenge here? Was that it?"

No answer.

"How about this, then? If I miss you six times, you're free." I grabbed her elbow, pulled her out of the seat ... and she sank to her knees once again, putting her head under my hand. My eyes widened as anger flared hot inside me. "Hey! Run!" I ordered, shaking her head as if it would wake her up. She buried her face in her hands, stifling sobs. "What?" I whispered. *"What?!"*

No answer.

"You're free!" I yelled. *"Go!"* I closed my fingers around the red-orange hair poking up between them, tilted her head back to look at her face: her skinned palms had smeared her cheeks with pink. Her eyes met mine: big, green, flecked with yellow. "What do you want from me?"

"I can't make it alone," she whined. "I couldn't even survive as a prostitute. That's why he threw me out. I don't know how to —"

I shoved her head, releasing her hair.

"The Mutation Edict is wrong," she scarcely whispered. "Wrong! You're letting me go ... you *must* see that it's wrong ...." Her pink tongue slid over her lips. "Please. Tell me so."

"Why?" I snapped. "What point does *that* serve?"

"Say it ... and you can Cap me," she whispered. "No false report to your bosses that I was unlocatable. No chance of getting caught for breaking your vows. You weren't working alone, right? I was thrown out and you were waiting for me! But, please, just say it ...!"

"You're nuts," I hissed. "Otherwise, you'd have gone to Mars in the first place. I should've kept that in mind right from the start." I nodded at her. "Move away from the car so I can finish this." I pointed the Enforcer at her, my elbow locked. "Now. Move!"

She shook her head, her only movement.

"Tryin' to turn me, aren't you?" I snapped. "Make me admit the law I've sworn to uphold is wrong?" My mouth curled into a sneer. *"No."* I shook my head. "I refuse. Cappers serve for life. Turned Cappers may as well be Mongos ...!" I pursed my lips. "I won't do it, Brid."

"You won't go through what I go through," she said slowly.

"No."

"You have a choice," she said. "I don't."

I nodded, reaching over her head to tug at the car door to get it closing to keep from staining my upholstery. "I'm just servin' my country," I repeated, stepping to the side so she would make less of a mess on my car. I checked to make sure my Enforcer was loaded —

It was *always* loaded when on a hunt. What was wrong with me?!

Still, when I looked down, she had not moved, her breath coming in gasps. She covered her face with her grubby fingers.

"I'm just servin' my country, Brid."

"Are you?" she asked, her voice muffled by her hands. "Capping Mongos is serving your country. You haven't called me a 'Mongo' in a while. You call me Brid." She lowered her hands and looked me in the eye. "So *am* I still a Mongo to you? If I'm not ... then this isn't Capping a Mongo —"

I pulled the trigger and she screamed, the sound nearly covered by the explosive discharge, then she sobbed brokenly. I reached under my trench coat and stuffed my Enforcer into the back of my pants again. I jerked her up to her feet with one hand and shoved her toward the UDX 5000. "I'll take you to Upper York, but then you're on your own. You walk away and I never see you again."

Words almost lost in a sob, she whispered, "Say the words ... pleeease ...!"

"The Mutation Edict is wrong?"

She looked up sharply, her nose and cheeks pink, her eyelids swollen, then she nodded.

"That's as close as you're gonna get." I started toward the other side of the UDX. "Now get in or I'm leaving without you." Both doors started to rise slowly, rotating on the forward hinges, and she climbed in even before I did. "No, here's one more." I extended my index finger, turned the back of my hand toward her, and stabbed it toward the sky. "Know what that means?"

"No," she scarcely whispered.

"It means 'up yours.' Especially if anybody mentions anything about you being in such good health. That's how Cappers report success: we cut off the right index finger at the middle joint and take it with us. Any mention at all, you give whoever it is a *big* 'up yours.' Prove you've got your whole finger. Understand?"

She nodded. "Thank you."

"*Now* that's all you get from me." I pressed the accelerator, starting the electric engine, and the doors started lowering back into position. "Not another word till we get there or I throw you out and see how well you fly without wings."

W.D. Kilpack III © 2024

DEAFENING CRIES

Teardrops from the skies
Wailing mourns
A distant drum rumbling
A thunderous striking pain

Heartbreak dawning like a crack of lightning
Through the rain
Another life taken
Spirit lifted to the sky
And so few who seem to care

Forsaken
Forgotten
Robbed

When will this crime end
Of all their sins
They can never be absolved
Resolutions made

Laws to uphold

Broken by the very ones elected

Beating us down,

Removing our faith,

Attempting to erase

Existence

Resistance is necessary

Or fates would be sealed

Someday, I pray, that hate will be repealed

Undo all the wrong

Break free

To see

The way they made

Isn't the way it was meant to be.

Sai Marie Johnson © 2024

QUANTUM PHYSICS AND GASSED CATS

---∞---

I'm trying to educate myself, so my mind doesn't end up like a bowl of grits. Sometimes, I sleep at night with my hands outside the covers and find myself thinking about stuff so much that I can't even get to sleep. Times like that, I just get up and turn on the computer and go to my favorite website, www.barelylegalbabesfordirtyoldmen.com.

Of course, looking at pictures of barely clothed babes in the middle of the night doesn't help me get to sleep but who cares as long as I'm having fun. Since I'm retired, it ain't like I have to get up and go to work. How do we know that looking at barely naked babes in the middle of the night ain't my job?

Generally, I don't go in for reading anything scientific, primarily due to the fact that there usually ain't no photos of naked babes. Yet, for some reason, this article about quantum physics held my attention for almost forty seconds. That, I believe, makes me an expert on the subject. I'm gonna explain it to y'all so you won't be ignorant on the subject like I was. Besides, it won't hurt you to read something educational for a change.

But I suppose I better warn you that nothing I say about this subject or any other would hold water any more than a pregnant woman after drinking a gallon of Gatorade. I am pretty sure none of you is smart enough to know anything about quantum physics because if you did, you sure as heck wouldn't be reading crap like this.

What is quantum physics? The term quantum is Latin for: '...How much of this theory is just plain B.S. It has something to do with discrete units that are assigned to specific physical quantities, such as the energy of an atom at rest. And we all know everyone, including atoms, should get plenty of rest.

Apparently, scientists wet their panties when they figured these waves could be measured in particle-like small packets of energy called 'quanta,' which started a bunch of grey-haired old geezers studying atomic and subatomic systems, which is now called *Quantum Mechanics*. These mechanics are really tiny little guys in jumpsuits running around with wrenches fixing protons.

There was something about how Newton's laws of motion couldn't explain something or other. Newton was never quite the same after that apple fell on his head, but he was a riot at office parties.

Most physicists believe quantum mechanics correctly describes the physical world under almost all circumstances except Hollywood. However, the effects of quantum mechanics are generally not significant when considering the observable Universe as a whole.

Dang that is some serious stuff, hey? As I read that, I could feel my sphincter muscles tightening. Frankly, I could care less if the orbit of the complex vectors gyrates around the probability of the uncertainty of the entire range of nucleus values, but what I do want to know is where do these freakin guys come from, the planet Vulcan? The deepest mystery I've ever thought about was how come when I eat corn, days later, I can see it clearly before I flush.

Curiosity or insomnia drove me on. I needed to know more about the kind of dudes that think this stuff up. That led me to this one guy, Erwin Rudolf Josef Alexander Schrödinger. With a name like that, it was clear he would either grow up to be a German Physicist or a serial killer. He was born in Edberg, Vienna, in 1887. His father was a cerecloth producer. I don't know what that was, so I'm going to just say he was a Hot Balloon Operator.

Growing up in 1887 in Austria there wasn't very much to do. There was no TV, computers, or Soccer; not even a decent war was raging. It is easy to see now that back then if you wanted something, you had to go out and invent it. Little Erwin was a frail, sickly kid who was the youngest of his five older sisters, Erwina, Ermelda, Erlisa, Ernada, and Erma, the oldest. If, in fact, he had any sisters, I'm sure that would be their names. They all mothered him, making him dress up like a girl and wear makeup as well as a whole bunch of other twisted, perverted stuff—probably. That's probably why, after he grew up, all the women he dated thought he was a 'nice guy,' but he could never get lucky.

In 1898, he attended the Akademische's Gymnasium, run by Mr. Akademische, but everyone called him Pops. This is where they assembled Arnold Schwarzenegger. Between 1906 and 1910, Schrödinger studied in Vienna under Franz Serafin Exner, a famous pastry chef.

Now if you haven't already stopped reading and went to the Web looking for www.barelylegalbabesfordirtyoldmen.com, this is where the story gets weird.

He began conducting experiments in the basement of the three-story walk-up where he lived. It is unknown what he was working on, but records show that he moved suddenly, and neighbors complained that an unusual number of pets went missing around the time he lived there. In 1911, Schrödinger had gained way too much weight and decided to get out of the bakery business and started looking for something where he wouldn't have to work weekends.

In 1914, Erwin Schrödinger achieved Habilitation (*venia legendi*). Okay, I'm guessing here, but I'm thinking that since he was Austrian, this must be some kind of classical piece of music he wrote. Obviously, it never made it to the top 100, and I think this is what forced him to become a commissioned officer in the Austrian Fortress Artillery. On April 6, 1920, Schrödinger married Annemarie Bertel. It was an arranged marriage. He arranged to have a cannonball dropped on his foot so he could be sent back home long enough to get hitched. In September 1921, after he had done a whole bunch of other crap, including getting married, he attained the position of full professor in Poland.

Schrödinger published in the school newspaper, *'Quantisierung als Eigenwertproblem.'* He was supposed to be writing a funny article on the food at the cafeteria, so the editor kicked him off the staff. However, the paper he wrote is now known as the *Schrödinger Equation*.

By now, if there is anyone reading this anymore, you must be saying like I did, "Who gives a flying fish?"

What most people don't know is that initially he named his paper *The Gertrude Equation*, after one of the waitresses at the 'Ratskeller,' but changed it after she married the drummer from the polka band. In this paper, he gave a 'derivation' of the wave equation for time-independent systems and showed that it gave the correct energy eigenvalues for the hydrogen-like atom. His paper has been universally celebrated as one of the most important achievements of the twentieth century since the invention of colored, glow-in-the-dark ribbed, flavored, latex condoms, or television if you ain't getting some. It created a revolution in quantum mechanics. What's really amazing was that he did it in study hall as he was looking over the shoulder of another student who was there on an athletic scholarship.

Another failing student hooked Schrödinger up with some really good drugs, and he went on to write the *Quantum Harmonic Oscillator, The Rigid Rotor,* (a manual for a marital aid) and *The Diatomic Molecule.* He never knew what was in those pills, but after that, he never wrote anything without a little toot or snort first. After he scored some more illicit substances, he wrote a new derivation of the *Schrödinger Equation,* a third paper in May showing the equivalence of his approach to that of Heisenberg and gave the treatment of the Stark effect.

A fourth paper in this most remarkable series showed how to treat problems in which the system changes with time, as in scattering problems. These papers were the central achievement of his career and were at once recognized as having great significance by the physics community, not to mention that he held the best fraternity parties in town.

At the University of Oxford, soon after he arrived, he received the Nobel Prize together with Paul Adrien Maurice Dirac. His position at Oxford, however, did not work out due to his unconventional personal life. Schrödinger living with two women, did not meet with acceptance. Hey, didn't I tell you this guy was a player?

In 1934, Schrödinger lectured at Princeton University; he was offered a permanent position there but did not accept it. Again, his wish to set up house with his wife and his mistress may have posed a problem. However, he was offered a deal to make an amateur adult film. He had the prospect of a position at the University of Edinburgh, but visa delays occurred, and in the end, he took up a position at the University of Graz in Austria in 1936.

The reason I really liked this guy Schrodinger is that he left Germany because he disliked the Nazis,' and he inspired the TV sitcom 'Three's Company,' (an American weekly show about a Nobel Peace Prize recipient in Quantum Physics who shared an apartment with a sassy brunette and a dim-witted blonde but never got none).

In 1938, after Hitler occupied Austria, Schrödinger had problems because of his flight from Germany in 1933 and his known opposition to Nazism. He issued a carefully weasel-worded statement saying that if Hitler wasn't a tyrannical dictator, held free elections, and shaved off that stupid mustache…he'd vote for him. He regretted this later when Einstein toilet-papered his house, and he had to apologize for being a wuss. However, the university had its own theory that all this amounted to a B.S. Degree, and I don't mean a Bachelor of Science. The faculty dismissed him from his job for political unreliability. He suffered harassment and received instructions not to leave the country, but he and his wife fled to Italy, seeking asylum and a really good pizza. From there he went to temporary positions at Oxford and Ghent Universities.

In 1940, he received an invitation to help establish an Institute for female alcoholics in Dublin, Ireland. He became the Director of the School for Theoretical Physics and remained there for seventeen happy years, during which time he became a naturalized Irish citizen. He wrote about fifty publications on various topics with pictures since it was easier to get 'lucky' with his magical 'charms' in Ireland.

In 1944, he wrote "*What is Life?*" for Reader's Digest (which contained *Negentropy*, concepts for genetic code), which wasn't whimsical enough to get published. Schrödinger stayed in Dublin until retiring in 1955. During this time, he remained committed to his particular passion: scandalous involvements with students where he fathered two children by two different Irish women. Geez, I'm wishing now I hadn't blown off all the science classes in college. In 1956, he returned to Vienna. At an important lecture during the World Energy Conference, he refused to speak on nuclear energy because of his skepticism about it and gave a philosophical lecture on swinging for married couples. During this period, Schrödinger turned from mainstream quantum mechanics' definition of wave-particle duality to promote the Bose Wave Radio, and decided to buy stock in the company, causing much controversy.

Speaking of controversy, the reason I spent so much time talking about Schrödinger is—that you have to understand the man...before you can understand his theories, and hopefully, I am getting paid 'per word' for this article. He is most noted for his theory called *Schrodinger's Cat*. Collecting cats presents a danger for the elderly. It starts with one itty-bitty kitty then grows to where old folks are up to their as…er…in cats, spending all their money on cans of tuna fish. Schrödinger must have suspected this in his later years when he tried to invent a cure. His theory went like this:

Schrödinger's Cat is a supposedly paradoxical thought experiment devised by Erwin Schrödinger (so everyone thinks) that attempts to illustrate the incompleteness of an early interpretation of quantum mechanics when going from subatomic to macroscopic systems. I believe in the scientific community that was supposed to be funny. The experiment proposes: A cat is placed in a sealed box. Attached to the box is an apparatus containing a radioactive nucleus and a canister of poison gas. This apparatus is separated from the cat in such a way that the cat can in no way interfere with it. The experiment is set up so that there is precisely a 50% chance of the nucleus decaying in one hour. If the nucleus decays, it will emit a particle that triggers the apparatus, which opens the canister and kills the cat. If the nucleus does not decay, then the cat remains alive. According to quantum mechanics, the unobserved nucleus is described as a superposition (meaning it exists partly as each simultaneously) of a 'decayed nucleus' and an 'undecayed nucleus.' However, when the box is opened, the experimenter sees only a 'decayed nucleus/dead cat' or an 'undecayed nucleus/living cat.'

This raises several questions:

- Where was he getting the cats for this experiment?
- If he was against the Nazis, why would his theory eerily be based on killing cats in a gas chamber?
- Was Schrodinger that dense or callous or just had crap for brains,' theoretically speaking?
- The most crucial question is: 'Where can I buy one of those devices…at Pet-smart or Pets Mart, I can never remember which it is.

In 1961, Schrödinger died and was buried in a huge crater, named Gertrude on the far side of the Moon.

I'm gonna miss him.

Grizzly G. Gus © 2025

THE GAZEBO

---∞---

The Northport Gazette, 1925, blared the headline: "PROMINENT CITIZEN PAUL MORTLOCK PERISHED IN PARK!" Paul, a man whose prominence was mostly self-proclaimed and based on his ownership of the town's only haberdashery, had met an untimely end beneath a grumpy gum tree in the local park. The circumstances were… unclear.

Some town folk whispered of a rogue cricket ball, others of a disgruntled cravat customer. Officially, it was ruled "death by misadventure," a catch-all phrase that covered everything from spontaneous combustion to tripping over one's own top hat.

To commemorate Paul (and perhaps to distract from the park's newfound reputation for lethal mishaps), the Northport Council, in their infinite wisdom, erected a gazebo. "The Paul Memorial Gazebo," a brass plaque declared. It was a fine structure, all wrought iron, and swirling flourishes, perfect for romantic trysts and avoiding sudden downpours.

Except for one slight problem: Paul.

Paul, despite his earthly demise, wasn't quite ready to leave Northport Park. He'd taken up residence in his gazebo. Not in a spooky, chain-rattling way, mind you. Paul was more of a spectral nuisance.

He'd clear his throat loudly just as a couple were about to share their first kiss.

He'd materialise a ghostly trilby hat on a young man's head, causing his sweetheart to shriek.

He'd even occasionally rearrange the decorative ironwork into suggestive shapes, much to the horror of elderly ladies enjoying their afternoon conversations.

Generations of Northport lovers grew up with tales of "Paul's Gazebo." It was a place to be avoided after dusk, a source of local legends, and a constant headache for the council, who received a steady stream of complaints about "unexplained breezes" and "phantom haberdashery."

Fast forward to 2025. Northport Park was still there, the gazebo still stood (albeit with a few more coats of paint), and the legend of Paul persisted.

One early evening, a woman named Betty was walking through the park when she was tragically mugged and killed. Betty, like Paul before her, found herself tethered to the park, her spirit unable to move on.

Betty, however, was a vastly different ghost than Paul.

While he was a fussy, slightly pompous spirit, Betty was a no-nonsense, modern woman. She quickly realised Paul's presence.

"Honestly, is clearing your throat? Is that the best you can do?" came Betty's voice.

Paul jumped. "Good heavens! Who… what…?"

"I'm Betty," she said. "And this," she gestured around the gazebo, "what you are doing is simply just ridiculous."

Paul replied: "I'll have you know this is a memorial! A tribute to a prominent…"

"A prominent haberdasher? Look, I get it. You're stuck. I'm stuck. But scaring teenagers and old ladies will solve nothing. Don't you agree?"

Over the next few weeks, an unlikely friendship blossomed between the two ghosts. Betty, with her modern sensibilities, helped Paul understand how his antics were perceived.

"You're not haunting," she explained, "you're just being a pest."

Paul told Betty about Northport's history, about the park's past, and about his own rather mundane life. He confessed that he wasn't prominent at all, simply a man who loved his shop and his town. He admitted he was scared and that he didn't know how to move on.

One evening, as the setting sun cast long shadows across the park, Betty had an idea. "Paul," she said, "we're both stuck here because we have unfinished business, right?"

"I suppose so," Paul replied. "But what business could I possibly have after all this time?"

"Closure," Betty said. "We need closure."

She proposed they work together to find peace.

Betty, having been a social media manager in her living life, suggested they use their combined spectral energy to project a message into the digital world. They focused their combined energy and sent a message to the Northport Historical Society, who were intrigued by the message and investigated the gazebo.

The historical society, after some research, uncovered the true story of Paul's death. It wasn't a cricket ball, or a disgruntled customer. It was a loose branch from the grumpy gum tree dislodged by a strong gust of wind. A simple accident.

The revelation brought Paul a sense of peace he hadn't felt in a century. He finally understood that his death wasn't some grand conspiracy or a cosmic joke. It was just… an accident.

For Betty, helping Paul allowed her to come to terms with her own sudden and violent death. She found solace in helping another spirit find peace and in connecting with the living world again.

This new clarification on Paul's death gave the town of Northport a fresh a new purpose. They placed a new and larger plaque, but this time it commemorated the town's resilience and did not mention Paul as a prominent citizen.

The council made a big deal of the news that had finally 'solved' the death of Paul Mortlock, but this time, the new plaque gave a history of the town.

When dusk fell on the evening of the ceremony, Paul, and Betty sensed a profound unburdening.

At last, they were free to cross over together into the eternal light.

José F. Nodar © 2025

SEVEN DAYS OF PICK ME UPS

Today is Sunday, and it's time for the day to begin,
Time to get ready for work again, just so the week can begin.
As the last day of the weekend fades away,
New challenges arise, but you'll find your way.
Never forget you have friends and family who care,
Just know you have many who are always there.
The weekend may be gone by the end of the night,
But don't let the week pass without finding delight.
The week starts tomorrow with all it brings,
But don't let it affect your joy and personal things.

Monday, the roughest day of the week,
Try not to feel too weak, or you'll falter by the end of the week.
The beginning is tough, but not the craziest of all,
Work may be hard, but home is your call.
To be there and then be home is a blessing to see,
Coming back to your community is where you're free.
Nothing to see, nothing to hear but the worries you may fear,
Just know it's only Monday; there's nothing to fear.

Tuesday is here, so it's time to persevere.
Be present in the moment, no matter where,
Work may be long, but time is on your side,
Never feel overwhelmed; let positivity be your guide.
Take things as they come, enjoy the good ahead,
Tomorrow will come, so rest easy in bed.

Wednesday is here, the middle of the week,
Stay strong, don't let yourself feel weak.
As the week drags on, it may feel longer,
But don't let that wear you down; you are stronger.
Things are what they are and will be,
But don't stress too much; let life flow naturally.
Talk to someone you hold dear,
Their support can make things clear.

Today is Thursday, but not a bird's day,
Every day brings lessons in its own way.
The workday may be long and draining,
But friends and community keep you sustaining.
Once you're home, you can finally unwind,
A drink in hand, with peace of mind.
Just know the day may have been stressful,
But home is where comfort is successful.

Today is Friday, and you can absolutely say yay,
With the weekend ahead, relaxation is on the way.
The week may have been long, but fun is near,
No need to worry, there's nothing to fear.
It is what it is, and it will be,
Surrounded by good friends and positivity.
Chill and relax, as the weekend will fly,
And soon enough, Monday will be nigh.
With Saturday so close, take time to adore her,
A moment to pamper, a moment to restore her.

Today is Saturday, a time to relax,
With fewer tasks and no need to act.
You have a stream tonight, but don't let it weigh,
Enjoy the moment, let your worries fade away.
A day of freedom, light, and delight,
Surrounded by love that shines so bright.
The struggles of the week may linger still,
But together with loved ones, you'll find the will.
In a world that sometimes feels unkind,
Find comfort in those who support you, heart, and mind.

Curtis L. L. Herbold © 2025

A HUNTER IN THE WILDERNESS

---∞---

In the heart of the sprawling, untamed wilderness, where the mountains kissed the sky and rivers roared with ancient wisdom, lived a seasoned hunter named Tuma. He was a man of the land, rugged and solitary, whose very essence seemed to be woven into the fabric of the wild. His life was one of survival, defined by the pursuit of game and the understanding of nature's subtle rhythms.

Tuma had hunted in these woods for as long as he could remember. The wilderness was his sanctuary, a place where he felt the pulse of the earth beneath his feet and the whisper of the wind in his ears. Every tree, every rock, and every river was an old friend, guiding him through the labyrinth of the wild.

One crisp autumn morning, Tuma set out on what he expected to be a routine hunt. His bow was slung over his shoulder, and his quiver full of arrows. The forest was alive with the sounds of rustling leaves and distant birdsong, but something felt different. There was an eerie stillness in the air, as if the wilderness was holding its breath, waiting for something unknown.

As Tuma moved deeper into the woods, the familiar trails seemed to vanish, replaced by a strange and unsettling terrain. The trees, once towering and majestic, now appeared twisted and gnarled, their branches reaching out like skeletal fingers. The underbrush grew thick and wild, making it difficult to navigate. Despite his unease, Tuma pressed on, driven by the hunter's instinct that something extraordinary awaited him.

Hours passed, and the sun began to sink behind the mountains, casting long shadows across the forest floor. Just as Tuma was about to turn back, he spotted movement in the distance. His heart quickened as he crouched low, moving silently through the underbrush. There, in a small clearing, stood a creature unlike any he had ever seen.

It was a massive stag, its antlers stretching high into the sky like a crown of twisted branches. Its fur shimmered with an otherworldly glow, and its eyes, deep and ancient, seemed to hold the wisdom of the ages. Tuma had heard legends of such creatures, whispered in the quiet of campfires, but he had never believed them to be true.

Slowly, he raised his bow, his hands steady and sure. But as he drew back the string, the stag turned its gaze upon him, and in that moment, Tuma felt a wave of understanding wash over him. This was no ordinary beast. It was a guardian of the wilderness, a creature as old as the earth itself, and to kill it would be to disturb the delicate balance of the wild.

Lowering his bow, Tuma knelt in the clearing, bowing his head in respect. The stag watched him for a long moment before turning and disappearing into the shadows of the forest, leaving Tuma alone with the fading light.

The wilderness was silent once more, but now it felt different. It was no longer a place to be conquered, but a world to be respected and revered. Tuma rose to his feet, his heart full of a newfound understanding. He turned and made his way back through the forest, his steps light and sure.

From that day on, Tuma was no longer just a hunter in the wilderness. He had become part of it, bound by a deep and unspoken connection to the wild, where the true heart of the earth beat in harmony with his own.

Damain Nakare II © 2025

WHEN THERE IS A WILL THERE IS A WAY

One day while I was sitting in my cubicle at my new office in the city of New Jersey where I was feeling a little out-of-place, I realized it was a good day to do lots of things. It was a strange sort of realization, because it was based more on a hunch and less on the element of routine. I usually was the type that got up and did things straightaway, but today the realization sort of dawned on me, and I was grateful, even in a strange sense, that it did.

I was not usually a lazy worker that did not like doing their work. I was new to the place, and I missed my home back in the countryside. While I sat there enjoying the grateful feeling, I noticed a picture on the wall. The picture said that "If there is a will there is a way" I liked this saying for some reason, and someone from the office staff had put up the beautiful light pink poster that had an ornate golden frame.

I thought about the saying, which I had heard about back in school, which was apparently four hundred years old. I happened to be an HSP with empath tendencies, so I had to do strange things to overcome some strange sort of jetlag that seemed to accompany everything I did. There was something to do that morning, and I was taking all my time, finding good enough reasons to be motivated enough to do it!

I seemed to have some sort of a photographic memory, so idioms like this stayed with me. They even gave me a strange sort of sense of direction. I felt lost at work, usually even though I was very intelligent and capable. I realized that this was a job that I might like doing, if I might find good enough reasons to do it, while putting in my best. Suddenly reality dawned on me, and I started to type the letter that needed to be completed as requested by my boss. I noticed there were lots of typos in the original document, and I had to proofread and edit all the stuff I was asked to redo for him. I also suddenly realized that my cell phone was ringing, and it seemed to be a call from someone I met at a coffee shop recently. A guy.

"Hello," I said,

"Hi" came back the beaming voice.

"Aren't you that guy I met at the coffee shop the other day?" I asked, as though I didn't know who he was.

"Yes, I'm also an artist, and those sketches you showed me the other day were remarkable," he replied with great admiration in his voice.

"Great, I can leave work early, as it's the weekend. Would you like to catch up?" he said again.

"Sure," I replied with a tinge of happiness in my voice.

I got back to my desk job and prepped myself to do as much as I could as fast as I could. Given that I was going to leave early, I started to think of ways to type quickly, never mind that there was indeed a lot to do. The boss knew I was good at proofreading, so he usually entrusted me with the usual load of paperwork.

Again, I looked at the picture on the wall. I typed what I could and had completed nearly 70% of the day's paperwork. I then, like the funny empath that I was, took a notepad that was close by and started to doodle. Given that I was a good artist, I thought about what my new date had said on the phone.

I had a black marker pen that I carried with me everywhere. I usually liked doodling, and I doodled like a 5-year-old, everywhere, on the books I read on the wall, like teeny tiny doodles, and even liked to draw fake tattoos on my hand.

I decided to draw one of the fake tattoos that I had drawn on a female friend ages ago. The tattoo was that of a cute but easy-to-recreate yacht in the middle of the sea that looked pretty cute on her, actually. She later went on to get a real ink tattoo of the same drawing with her boyfriend's name underneath it.

I easily recreated the same drawing, and this time I wrote the text that was on the wall beneath it. The beautiful rough sketch looked resplendent with the words "When there is a will, there is a way" written so eloquently underneath.

I got back to the paperwork and completed my daily office routine, but left early as it was the weekend. I called up the guy I was supposed to be meeting, and he said he was in the vicinity. We caught up at the same coffee shop that we were so used to visiting, because of its beautiful aura and authentically Asian menu. There he was in the restaurant, being himself, the last time I remember him. His hair was auburn, and his eyes were blue. He looked every bit the artist that "loved what they did, and hence did not really work a day in their life" I sat down opposite him at the table and noticed that he had already ordered a tall glass of mocha latte for me.

"You are new to the City of New Jersey. That's what you told me the last time we met," he said in one long sentence without stopping.

"Yes, and I feel like the City is giving me great vibes, but it's taking me a while to get used to things!" I replied with an honest look on my face.

He saw the sketch I made in the notebook I got from work and was amazed.

"I think the drawing has captured the essence of the phrase very well" I think you would make a great artist too, by the way. I want to get this framed. I will put it up in my home, in my drawing room. Also, don't feel as lost as you do in the city of New Jersey! That's coz "When There is a Will there is a way" and you have found a friend in me as well!

That day I went home and thought about the reason for liking the 400-year-old idiom. I was the type 'that never got around' and I always had to start things from scratch to get them to work. I thought about the kindly artist's words, and the fact that he simply adored my doodle, and wanted to get it framed. For now, things were going somewhere, and I had found a friend in the big city. Probably the saying was true. And if I had a will to do things, there would be a way to do them.

Sarah Desouza © 2024

FIRST DECISION

───────── ∞ ─────────

Fred now had the ship all to itself after the shuttle left the back bay to make a somewhat dangerous delivery to the planet below. Being able to check on things from anywhere, as Fred was a part of the ship in many ways, it went to go to the galley and kitchen area first. Fred had done a lot of research on the strange process that organics were required to intake outside items to maintain their existence. Fred added the information to the archives of its memory banks the facts that humans developed what they call taste or appeal to the items they ingested. It was in Fred's original programming to do whatever it could do best at any time, so as a free and learning AI, it looked for items in the food processing duplicator to please it friends. Fred was illegal as a free AI.

Originally Fred was developed to be part of the ship, a limited AI to assist the human pilot. The original owner had been lazy and had not kept a neat ship. So, he bought the empty robot body and had the ship's program installed. This allowed him to give it orders to handle the loading for his small deliveries.

Although there were lots of items in its programming that was automatic, at times, the slovenly owner would have to type in instructions to get something different handled by the robot with the round head. This lazy man threw discarded food platters and cups wherever he went or sat. The smell on the ship was only met by the body odor of the owner.

But a drunken landing let the ship drop through tangled electrical wires, and a building with conduits that allowed a power surge to wipe everything inside the cruiser clear. The ship was put up for sale cheaply as it needed a good cleaning and a lot of rewiring. When it was restarted by Brian, the lady who bought it, the robot was also restarted. She had done a lot of re-wiring, using a new modern type of connection and not having to crawl through the walls with the long spools of actual wire. Connections sent contacts from point to point and eliminated interference which could be replaced easily.

As the new owner, Brian, was checking out the Robot. She turned on all of its abilities but did not engage the control on AI learning. Uncontrolled AIs were illegal on some worlds as there was the thought that artificial life could become more intelligent than humans and take over. Being an ex-sergeant from the military and having worked on the battlefields with self-sufficient robots, Brian did not have uncomfortable doubts about robots that could learn and act. In fact, she felt there was an advantage to having someone to talk to on the long trips she was going to make in her new job as a lone delivery ship owner.

For Captain Brian McDagoon, cleaning up her ship and getting it ready for space, the robot was a big help and able to do additional things as it learned from her. She smiled as the robot found tools to add to its body to make it better to help her repair the ship. When the robot sat still on extended rollers on the floor, it was a large oval body with an attached round head sitting on top. The head had a narrow grill that circled it all the way around over two-thirds of the way up, and the robot had explained this was a visual view that gave it 360% options all the time. A flat grill was where sounds emitted, so Brian considered that was the point where the robot looked at her or something, the front of the face.

It wasn't long before the robot archived the information that the Captain had given it a name, and inside its archives, it had strange issues that it studied that humans had names, so it was called Fred. What happened was Fred learned and learned and acquired masses of knowledge that it continued to retain. With its strong power from the ship it could instantly pull from all of these statistics. This was how it made a selection, using math and percentage of failure on what to select. There was so much out there to discover, and there was so much that it could do to help the Captain.

One of the things Fred did was to begin building very small cleaning robots. The Captain approved of the small round cleaners with the ability to sweep, suck up debris and disappear into small built-in wall slots. After a while, it was common to always see one or another of the cleaners on a wall or window.

It was like the many tools and now some weapons that were hidden behind the smooth exterior of the large body of the robot. Small doors could pop open or slide down and out would pop the most amazing extension that the robot had created for itself. These did not disturb Brian as she always felt they were there to support her more than the robot itself. The ability to achieve such devices came from watching old vids and what ancients people used to clean. Calculating the amount of time saved by having the small units keeping the ship cleaned and opening up the ability to more time learning let the math percentages show an advantage for the Captain. The ability to take from the pile of old junk in the storage bay and build the small cleaning bots was part in Fred's programming and part new archives on what human's used to maintain their abodes.

Being in the galley was a schedule in Fred's archives and part instructions from Fred's Captain, to often prepare meals. The bot found it interesting and looked up cooking instructions and recipes all the time to please the human. The robot was working on the noodles for lasagna when it got the warning from the shuttle that something was wrong.

Tuning into the main speaker on the dashboard, as he ignored gravity and floated at a fast speed to the bridge, he spoke to the Captain.

"Come in, Captain. Repeat your words. Contact is faint." Fred reached the bridge and began to work on the dashboard to bring up a different speaker.

The speaker was full of static, and the Captain's voice was faint. "It was a trap. Help us, Fred." There were some other words, but they were too faint, and the static distorted them so that Fred couldn't understand them. Not wanting to waste any time, the robot did two things at the same time. First, the robot began to move the spaceship in its orbit to a position that would take it closer to the city of Palimar, and then it checked on the condition of the shuttle. Second, Fred's direct contact with the distant shuttle needed to be upgraded, as Brian had been in the pilot's seat on the trip down to the planet.

Once Fred had fully inserted itself into the dashboard of the shuttle, there was an entirely different amount of information coming in. There were no outside cameras on the shuttle, but Fred had enough power to find that the shuttle was being rocked by outside weapon fire. Checking on the inside shuttle views, most were tilted or contained a lot of static. At last, Fred got a vision of its friend, the Captain, lying on her back just past the inside door lock. This was the standard airlock system with an outside door and an inside door. There was a small safe waiting area in between to either hold air or expunge it, depending on the conditions. The outside door was closed.

Giving a movement through the system, the bot got the inside shuttle door closed and locked. Running a scan of the shuttle,

Fred realized that the other human was not on board. But Fred was tied in some deep electronic connections about the Captain and weighed options to bring the shuttle up and get her some medical treatment and then take the shuttle down and try to help the other human, who was a unique warrior. The man might be unusual, but Fred still had records that the man was important to save, and Fred would do what the Captain wanted.

The robot would have preferred to be in the bay when the shuttle arrived, as Fred was worried about the injuries to the robot's friend. But to handle a moving object when it was not onboard, Fred needed to be on the bridge of the spaceship. There, Fred had all the power of the magnets, hooks, and pulls to handle, bringing in something to a bay.

Fred used the larger bay, had several haulers move everything out of the way, and lifted the shuttled off the ground to come up at an angle through the atmosphere. The robot had to bring up some special programming to make sure it knew how to move the shuttle through the atmosphere safely.

The robot's body, which generally was smooth and oblong, was now showing all types of extensions as doors and covers slid open. It gave the robot the look of some type of unfinished metal monster. An observer would think that the machine had gone out of direction, with some of the extension rods with small pointers speeding over dials and a shining keyboard, but some injected into the dashboard.

On a screen were multiple views; of the bay, the back camera that was locked on the distant shuttle, a camera on the top of the shuttle that was tilted, and one still on the unmoving Brian McDagoon. For a robot that could work in microseconds, the long time it took to carefully protect the human body in the shuttle meant a slow delivery out of the planet's gravity and into the large back bay seemed hard to put together in human time.

At last, having everything stabilized, Fred flew through the narrow halls and leaped to the floor of the bay. Using the robot's electronic built-in commands of the shuttle, it opened the side door lock, both the outside and the inside, as it floated up and settled down near the silent body.

Extending a tool that could detect temperature, Fred found that Brian was a bit warm for the standard human condition. Fred took a second to bring up some information on human medical conditions. The robot had millions of files to compare, but cut off most of the information, needing to find something to let it help the woman. To begin with, the first warning was not to move the patient until what might be wrong, such as head wounds, broken bones, and internal injuries. Instead, information flashed by, and Fred floated over to Brian's head and extended two arms with soft coverings on the ends.

Feeling Brian's neck in the correct place, Fred bobbed away in what could be called happiness to feel the pulse. She was alive.

But dropping back down, now it was essential to keep her that way. So Fred had to get such a great friend out of the shuttle and up to the med room.

All the beginning tutorials said not to move the injured, but Fred knew that to save this friend, she would have to be taken to the med room. There the limited med doc programs would give details and provide healing progress. They had more precise information built into their programs on the human system and were meant to handle injuries.

Going out of the shuttle, Fred began to hunt for what would handle the woman with the least amount of movement. Locating a plate piece of metal on a side wall that was the right size, Fred had repair robots remove it and place it on a small hauler. Returning to the shuttle, instructing the hauler carefully, Fred helped slide the metal under Brian and lifted her, almost with no moves, off the shuttle and out into the bay. Using the large loading elevator, they got their precious cargo up to the main cabin floor and into the med room.

Using only the soft covers on the extension arms, Fred very carefully pulled Brian off the metal slab and onto the flat med bed. Ignoring the hauler, Fred only needed to spin around in the close quarters and hit the buttons that activated the limited medical AI. A blue light scanner came on and began to slowly move down from head to toe of the woman's body. Up on a screen, a human skeleton was forming, and specific places were turning red with information forming below on another screen.

Arms began coming out, and they started removing her clothing, first taking off her boots, then actually cutting the clothes to pull them away. Reading the information on the bottom screen was where the critical data about the injury appeared; Fred was collecting info fast.

She had been shot in the leg with a slug thrower, and the small metal was still there. It could be safely removed, and that action was advised. Fred tapped approval.

But the blue scan had returned to Brian's head, and now a tiny white light was also pointing down just above where it had been bleeding. Looking at the readout, Fred found there was nothing to tap. The last sentence was the one that put Fred into a dilemma that was not covered in his programs or archives.

UNABLE TO PERFORM NECESSARY CORRECTION TO PATIENT.

That meant that Brian needed to be transported to a hospital where her head wound could be treated by surgeons. But Fred would have to leave the other human Drak down on the planet if it moved the ship to save Brian.

Fred had to make a decision. This was an alien word to an AI that hard started out as a ship's computer. Oh, Fred new the dictionary meaning, the robot had several dictionaries on file. The first dictionary noun said: a conclusion or resolution reached after consideration.

Robots, or more important the unleashed AI didn't consider or resolve problems, they researched through previous actions and correlations and compared tables and percentages of results. Fred's Captain had not put restrictions on it, the original programs had. It was a slow learning process for Fred to grow beyond that beginning dictate. In comparison to human time, Fred's ability to research, calculate, evaluate, quantify, assess percentages, calibrate and find that the word decision was inside the human. They called it a quick reaction to pressure or emotions leading them or the Captain would say she just had a gut feeling to make a decision.

This was one of the rare commodities that set sentient beings alive and different from built devices, This was not the usual choice that Fred faced. They weren't really decisions, but they needed to be weighed quickly, all the facts and options and choose the right option. Fred watched hours of human videos and movies while the robot was not on duty or the humans were sleeping. Fred saw the different times when in some particular problem, a man or woman had to make a decision, and sometimes, they made the wrong decision. Fred would quietly shout out when they knew the wrong decision was going to get the hero in the show in trouble. Decisions were a learning process, not something that could be found in the books or the archives. It had never been part of the robot's original programming, and it had not been learned before now.

Instantaneously, fields of information ran through the different memory chips and gamma atoms that were held in stasis. Unfortunately, much of the AI's ability was not in a solid state. An uncontrolled learning robot had to have a lot of additional areas to store and find information. But there were so many places to find and study, from personal peoples' storage areas to the great public information regions that were sliding loose across systems and planets.

Fred understood what the word decision meant because the meaning was available in many dictionaries. But it had never been part of his programs. This was a learning process that the Captain had not covered when they discussed so many things as they traveled. Fred could sit here for hours or years and study the word and never understand it until faced with the action. Now the robot was faced with action. Humans made decisions all the time, but robots were programmed with choices. Fred looked at the unconscious woman and moved.

Instructing the med room to provide a secure cover for Brian on the examining bed, Fred flew out of the room and began to grab items from different closets as the bot headed to a side unit that was seldom used. It contained escape pods. A human would have said that the mind was in turmoil, trying to cover everything at once.

Getting the escape pod door open before he approached, he put in weapons, extra food, and a message to Drak. The message was simple, "We will return for you."

Putting a dirty shirt of Drak's in the pod would let Drak be able to open the pod. With that, Fred sent it off to land in the same place where the shuttle had set down. The best hope was that Drak, who had special abilities, would find ways to survive and perhaps find the message. There might be a good chance for the Veldan Warrior to survive until they could return for him.

Now the bot was ready to get to the nearest hospital as fast as possible. Fred had made a decision.

M. Garnet © 2025

IT CUTS DEEP

The silence is deafening.

Every sunrise seems to bring another story, another stolen sister, another daughter ripped from the heart of our community.

This genocide, this plague of violence against our Indigenous women, girls, and Two-Spirits, tears at the very fabric of our existence.

In the face of this horror, some might say it's us versus them.

But in the quiet corners of the internet, in the shared tears and outrage on social media, a different story unfolds. Here, connections blossom, unexpected bridges are built.

Biracial and White sisters reach out, yearning to reconnect with their roots, hearts heavy with the weight of history.

They offer their skills, their voices, their very selves to the fight.

It cuts deep, the sting of rejection.

To be told your pain isn't real, your desire to help just a performance.

We are all hurting, all yearning for the day this violence ends.

Who are we to turn away a helping hand, even if its skin doesn't match our own?

This isn't about trophies or accolades.

This is about unity, about a tapestry woven from the threads of our shared grief and unwavering determination.

Every voice matters, every connection amplifies the cries of our missing sisters.

Yes, there will be those who exploit tragedy for their own gain.

We must be wary, but let's not drown out the chorus of genuine support with suspicion.

Let's not chase away allies in the very hour we need them most.

Let this social media web we weave not be a net of exclusion, but a net of strength, a net that catches and lifts us all.

Every tear, every share, every connection is a prayer for justice, a whispered promise to the ancestors, to our stolen sisters, that we will not rest until they are all brought home.

Don't silence the voices that rise in support.

Let them join ours, and together, let us drown out the deafening silence with the roar of a united movement.

Sai Marie Johnson © 2025

THE UNSEEN

I wake up, my head scolding me for such impertinence. The sun streams into my apartment through the open window, as if extending a hand of warm friendship.

Damn sun!

I peer reluctantly around my room, wondering what I did last night. It doesn't take Sherlock Holmes to paint a sorry picture from the half-chewed pizza slice slumping on the table and the empty bottle of bourbon lying open on the floor.

Once I was a painter, the artist kind not the tradesman kind. Not successful, not yet, but on my way up. Or at least I thought so. I believed that life should be grasped, that nothing was more important than the work we choose to carve our own identity into an otherwise indifferent reality. Almost nothing. My life was one of struggle, yet one filled with the joys of potential and growth. If my work was my passion, the friends I collected along the road were my love. Not the food of life, but the spice. Not just spice, but a rare and wonderful one.

What a fool.

When my wife died, I died. Our love was an expression of us both, of our totality, our work and our life and our dreams. The work could not survive her loss. The hope and fire became ashes with her.

At some level, I know I should get over this. Never fully over it but placing it gently in its own sacred room, where I could treasure and revisit it without being ruled and ruined by it. While my life and work go on. I know it is what I should do. I know it is what she would have wished. But I cannot. It is if a dim film lies over the world I once loved, and it can no longer reach me. I still meet my friends, occasionally. But they can no longer touch me either.

I do not need to work, not for a long time. My wife, ever more prudent than I, was careful to maintain a healthy insurance policy in case something happened to her, never believing it would. For whom does? And yet it did. A mistake. I still need to eat and drink, as the pizza and liquor attest so eloquently. Perhaps if I still had to work, I would work and work myself back into myself. There can be a fine line between prudence and folly, though I know it is I who corrupted one into the other.

I know this is self-pity. But the knowledge brings no power to overcome it.

I feel a sudden rebellion against the mess and scraps and smells, attempt to make myself slightly presentable in some feeble echo of past pride, and head down to the street.

I smile amiably at the doorman as I pass, but he ignores me, staring stonily ahead as if I am not here. I wonder what I did to him to offend him so but lack sufficient desire to find out. As I turn, I gently bump a passerby. But instead of the expected gruff "watch it!" he just shakes himself and moves on, as if my existence is beneath his notice in his busy private world.

There is something strange about the people I pass. I am used to the way pedestrians on a busy street ignore each other, but it is both more and less than that. It is like they do not even see me. Even if I smile at them, I get neither smiles nor scowls in return, just blank indifference. Yet if I am in their way, they pass around me, without acknowledging my presence.

Weird.

What was that thing I read about once? Blindsight? An affliction in which a person reacts to what they see, yet are not conscious of seeing it? It is as if the world has become blind sighted. Do they see each other? Yes, I see people greet each other, talk to each other, farewell each other, even argue. It is only me they do not see.

I smile grimly to myself, remembering my thoughts about the dim film I have cast over a world I no longer truly see or care for. Perhaps the world is now returning the favour.

I shiver. Get a grip!

Then I laugh at my own delusions. Somebody must.

I pick a breakfast spot at random, so unfairly offended at the world that I'd rather meet new strangers than risk old acquaintances. I sit down and try to attract the attention of the waitress, but she ignores me, the amount of her tip dropping by the minute. As she passes, I touch her arm, but instead of turning to me, she shakes her arm and moves on: not annoyed, not even puzzled, just reacting to a half-felt touch that didn't reach her awareness. Like a cat twitching its tail at an unwanted contact from something beneath its dignity to notice.

Though there are empty tables, a man sits down opposite me, ignoring me like everybody else. I start getting annoyed but then decide to just run with this strange day and test its limits. I stare at him, but he doesn't flinch. I pick up a piece of his bacon and chew it, glaring at him challengingly, but he doesn't react to the insult. I even take his coffee out of his hand and drink some, but while he looks a little puzzled to then find it sitting on the table, he just picks it up again and resumes drinking. I am tempted to spit in the damn thing.

I poke him in the chest, but he reacts no more than the waitress when I touched her arm. I wonder how he would react if I stabbed him with a knife, but I decide I'm not ready for such drastic action. He'd probably just think he'd somehow stabbed himself!

Suddenly panic constricts my chest and I run. I leave a trail of disturbed people in my wake, but the most reaction I get is when two of them think they bumped each other and start quarrelling.

I lean with my back to a wall, panting heavily, seeing the crowd who cannot see or even feel me, only the wake of my passage: as if an invisible ship cleaved their ocean but all they see are impersonal waves fleetingly rocking their existence.

Then it dawns on me. The strangeness and contradictions finally worm their way into my own consciousness, and I realise this is a dream. Have you not had the same experience? A dream drifting into the shallows of your mind until you realise its nature, and once named, vanishes?

But the wall resolutely remains a wall, the crowd continues going about its business. If this is a dream, then it will not let me go.

I wander around until it is dark, stealing food when I am hungry and drinks when I am thirsty. What else can I do, when nobody can see me to accept payment? I wonder if I can enjoy myself. There is a snooty nightclub. In my rising career,

I might have gained entry. Now, no way, yet I just waltz in without challenge. I taste a few expensive drinks, dance before a few attractive girls, mesmerised by their rhythm and what it does to their bodies. I see a couple smile at each other, take each other's hands, and leave. I could follow them, and they would be none the wiser, but I cringe from such invasion of privacy. A flame of lust hits me, and I realise I could follow any of these women home, and I wonder what they would do, how they would react and explain it, if I were to have my unseen way with them?

Some have said that we are moral only out of fear of being caught, and who can punish the unseen man? But they are wrong. Perhaps it is their own selves they are describing. While I feel I have lost myself, I find that I have not. I would never have violated someone's rights so terribly before. If I did it now, my wife's ghost would despise me. My own soul would despise me. Then I would truly be lost.

***

It is early morning. I am walking along the beach, feeling the cool breeze off the ocean, relating to the mournful cry of lonely gulls, attempting to feel the beauty of the growing dawn, yet feeling that too is beyond me.

I like the emptiness and peace. I hate the crowds who cannot see me. If I am to be alone for the rest of my days, I prefer to be truly alone, just me wandering an empty world.

So, I feel a twinge of annoyance when I see a man sleeping on my beach, wrapped in some ratty cloak, as if he had dropped there in despair yet still held a hope of the dawn to come. He seems to sum up my own existence: a lonely body, alone on an empty beach, no future or past, just a life washed up on an infinite and uncaring shore. I approach him and look down upon him.

I feel a savage desire to kick him just to watch him react, but I recoil from my own incipient cruelty. Such thoughts are strange to me, and I wonder if I am losing my soul. What then will be left of me? Perhaps when I betray the last of me, my body will dissolve into mist, and I will at last be free of this curse where I exist without leaving a mark or a ripple in others' minds. But I cannot betray the last of me. Not yet. Something still holds me to this Earth. So, I gaze upon this stranger's face, wondering what story his life holds and what led him here, knowing I can never know.

He opens his eyes.

***

I awaken on the beach, to find a woman staring down at me. She is young, raven-haired, attractive in a purposeful if somewhat lost way, her eyes a living blue peering between long black lashes.

Eyes that are alive, boring into mine, not filmed and unseeing. I am too startled to be cautious, and cry out, "You can see me?"

Her eyes widen and she replies, "You can see me?"

If not for her strange echo—and if I were dreaming, how am I on the beach I lay down on in that dream?—I might have thought I had finally awakened. Yet I remain cautious, not wanting to graduate from dreaming to being locked up for my own good.

"What do you mean?" I ask.

"You know what I mean!" she snaps. She is either more courageous than I, or more desperate.

We stare at each other for long moments, until she asks forlornly, "Do you think we're dead?"

"I don't think we're dead. No body, no obituary. And who heard of ghosts having to eat?"

She sits down next to me with a sigh. "What has happened to us?" she asks in a small voice. I can only shake my head. For now, we feel no need to introduce ourselves, no need to relate our life stories. For now, it is enough to be together and watch the sun rise flaming above the waves.

***

Weeks have passed, weeks as vague as a dream, yet filled with a sharp sweetness.

Perhaps I am in love. This man I found on a beach, so shattered, yet retaining some indomitable strength that while beaten down remains waiting to reassert itself, has reached my soul in a way no other has. He too seems to be healing. He now looks at the beauty of trees, sunsets, streets and people as if not passively accepting their glory, but itching to take it, express it, improve it and make it his own. He said he was once an artist. Now when he is lost in contemplation, I see his fingers twitching, as if holding an invisible brush.

And I see in his eyes a reflection of the feeling in mine.

Finally, one night he reaches for me, and we make love where we are, on the beach, in sight of the whole world if only it could see us, without guilt or regret. As I gaze on his sleeping face, I wonder if one day we shall have a child, but tremble at the thought. Would they inherit our curse? Or worse, never be able to see us or feel our touch? Never know we were. I shudder, then I too am asleep.

***

I wake with a start in my own room, no longer on the sand. No longer with her. I look around and see that even the fungus has given up on my old pizza.

Something ineffable has changed. The world feels real, pungently tangible again.

I see my dried-out paintbrushes, and for the first time in so long, feel the need to again express the inexpressible. I think of my wife and find her where she would want to be: in my soul, in that room where I can visit her, but in my past, not coating my present with impossible regret. I think of what I have won.

Then I remember a dark-haired dream lover, and think of what I have lost.

I head downstairs, and the doorman greets me. The world, so long shrouded in mist, seems bright and alive with promise. I smile at people in the street, and some of them smile back. I laugh in simple abandon, and some people grin at me, others pull back nervously. That just makes me laugh the more.

I order my breakfast, sip my coffee and lean back, closing my eyes in melancholy contentment. I feel someone sit down opposite me and open my eyes at the intrusion.

Her bright blue eyes look at me through her long lashes, and I smile.

Robin Craig © 2025

ABOUT MY SIGHT

Let me tell you something about my eyes.

Yes, they are brown and nothing more dazzling there to find.

As basic as can be but nothing is basic about the ability to see.

There are a few things on earth that have crossed my eyes viewed by very few and have shaped my humanity.

The suffering of a parent on the border of life-altering surgery.

A face devoid of hope when depression hinders abilities.

The light found when friends turn to lovers for the first time.

Then the surprise they find as they look at everything they can now call mine.

The rise of fools to soldiers that look at death with a calm face.

The change of heart from a boss that believed they would only leave others disgraced.

The overwhelming joy from a joke that you can giggle at for several minutes.

The want for the one person to arrive to a party when everyone else is in it.

The one thing I long to see now is the sky.

It's a simple thing but complex for me, permit me to tell you why.

When I look up, I have 10 seconds before my tears well up and my eyes slam shut.

Working in darkness and with long spans of computer screens will also leave your eyes also wishing you could look up.

I can do so if I lie on my back.

Looking forward to the horizon and hopefully not needing a hat.

Tell me what's up there so I may dream as you do by day.

From there look into my eyes, can you see what they are trying to say?

The Paper Man © 2023

THREADS

I've always been self-destructive. The kind of person who will pick at scabs and pull at loose threads, without realising that, sooner or later, everything will unravel, fall apart and leave me bleeding.

This is a final confession, a list of the stupid things I did and how they led to my death. A list of the threads I kept on pulling and how they fell apart.

The first was my mother. I tugged at her patience throughout my life and eventually, it unravelled.

You see, it was always just my mother and me. There never was any greater concept of family. We had one another and that was supposed to be enough. But of course, it wasn't. I pulled at the threads of her patience, asking her endless questions about why it was just us. The kids at school all I had fathers, or stepfathers, or aunts and uncles that helped out. Why didn't I?

Eventually, the threads snapped, and she lost patience with me. The alcohol didn't help, it probably wore her patience thin. I remember her drunken yelling, the blows…

The neighbours must have been able to hear her as well, because someone called the police. There was a social worker, a strange, scatty woman who tried too hard to be my friend. She took me away from my home and I lived in a sort of orphanage for a while, but still, I insisted on pulling at a new thread. Well, in many ways, it was the same one, just a different strand. The strand that connected me to my unknown father.

I was adamant that I wasn't an orphan, so I did as much research as I could and eventually, I tracked him down. At first, the man wanted nothing to do with me, but I'm nothing if not persistent. Especially when I shouldn't be.

I kept in contact with him, stubbornly writing emails, texts and letters. As he blocked my numbers and email addresses, as I watched through the window while he tore my letters in two, I planned new ways to get in touch with him. Fake numbers I could use. Places where I could accidentally stumble across him.

Yes, in many ways, I became a stalker. But even as it dawned on me that what I was doing was insane, I continued desperately. Even as I realised that everything I had would fall apart again, I kept pulling at the threads, like some neurotic kid following their obsessive cycle, biting at nails and picking at scabs.

But the threads of my father's patience didn't fall apart as violently as my mother's. He didn't turn on me when they snapped, but instead, he seemed to take pity on me. He agreed to spend time with me.

We used to have our awkward little chats in a coffee shop near his house. For an hour or two, it would feel like we were normal. We'd sit down and talk. He would tell me about work and his – my – extended family. And I, feeling like I finally had everything I ever wanted, a complete and ordinary family, was careful, for once in my life. I kept the clumsy questions about my mother and their past together bottled up in my head.

The awkwardness soon passed. I felt like my father truly cared for me. If not as his daughter, then as his friend. And I cared for him. No, more than that, I worshipped him, simply for treating me with some dignity, after everything we had been through.

But what leads one to pull at loose threads if not curiosity? A sense that they shouldn't, perhaps? I had both. So of course, it was inevitable that one day, I would ask the forbidden question, knowing as I did that I was throwing away everything I had spent my childhood dreaming of.

His face was blank and impassive as I spoke of my mother. I asked him all the questions on my mind. How had he met her?

Did he still love her? Was she an alcoholic then? Was she violent? Did he know—

Eventually, he cut me off. He looked up at me with cold, empty eyes and told me it was time for me to leave.

I knew then, as I stood up with tears in my eyes, that I wouldn't see him again. It was history repeating itself.

This time, I didn't have the energy to chase him around and beg him to charge his mind. I hardly had the energy to do anything. And I certainly didn't have the time. Because I was eighteen now, and that's when the system stops caring about the children 'rescued' from homes. I had to leave the children's home and since I had nothing and no one else left, all my free time was spent searching desperately for a job.

However, my rescue came in a completely different, miraculous form. While hunting for a job, I met Thomas. He was handsome, rich and, amazingly, interested in me. Within a month, we were living together in his beautiful apartment. I could hardly believe my luck.

But of course, I had to ruin it, like I ruined everything else. I began to pull at his life as well, with a kind of crazed curiosity. I was trying to find something to reassure me that he actually liked me. After all, we were worlds apart. He had no reason to care for me.

What I actually found was where he went when I wasn't home. The hotel Nikti was an interesting place. There were always a lot of pretty young women there, for one thing. In his room.

Another beautiful thing destroyed by mindless pulling at threads.

There is another interesting thing about threads, you know? A thread is such a tiny, fragile thing… Like me. But when it's wound around someone's neck, it has the power to destroy.

My mother. My father. Thomas. I called them my threads. But the only threads in my life that didn't snap were the ones around all their necks.

Ellie Jay © 2025

EPICURUS THE BUDDHA

―――∞―――

A woman's laughter and a man's mockery slow down his dance.

But they don't stop it. He joins in their laughter.

With a gesture, he invites them to dance.

An attempt that often fails and he repeats with hope.

He goes back to his thing, which is dancing. Let others speak.

Especially those who observe to be shocked and disapproved.

There is nothing good for those paralyzed by the tongue and its judgments.

At some point they will see that they are talking to no one and will remain silent.

He continues dancing, which is his thing.

He moves without expectations.

He doesn't plan or do too many calculations. He lacks nothing.

He urges no one or gives instructions.

One can only do what one is, he seems to tell us.

Incapable of hating, he heals his wounds and that's it.

He doesn't blame the truces of the exhausted.

Nor the obstacles of the half-living, incapable of burning.

They lack half of the dance.

In the direction of the figure, the stones fly. The usual.

They are leftovers of indigestible food that do not even touch it.

Stupidity always awaits a response. If there is not one, it is its defeat.

There is no rebound because there was no blow.

These stones join the dance, they exalt it.

There is no stoned dancer, but only dance.

He pays attention to us for the seconds that last his failed invitation.

He is not going to waste time with children who refuse to grow.

The blind man will cure his blindness!, the dance shouts, and he smiles as he moves.

He cannot love like us. He does not understand what we are referring to.

Ours why and ours when. There is no manual or instructor beyond himself.

He savors the sweet, swallows the bitter.

Without complaints or spills, he is a transmuter.

If it is a matter of preferences, and if he loves something,

it is the middle ground that moves him.

He dives into the recesses of those foreign bodies, where he always drowns.

His drowned face shines, returning from the depths.

Like Poseidon, he generates earthquakes, he tames horses.

He loves until the last drop, if that is what it is about.

Loving, he disappears, as when he dances.

He does not say it. It would be unnecessary, confusing.

He drags it with him, he enjoys it and that is enough.

Why mention the volatile, if the dance of life is at hand?

One could swear: he is not one of us.

He is not circumscribed to himself, reduced and apocryphal.

He does not expect anything, nor calculate. He does not compare.

Nor does he jump from one desire to another unbridledly.

What he seeks or has already found is not there.

His dance, his songs, his cries like sparks that ignite, are neither visible nor heard.

The stones they throw at him are not necessarily rocky.

He is not there even if we see him, it is a form he uses. One more, among many.

He walks naked or elegant. He complies with what has been imposed on him.

Without wearing himself out.

He saves strength to continue dancing. To drown in anybody and love until he dries up. And then continue shining.

We will never discover it, unfortunately.

We lack depth in our gaze. Inner lights, trackers.

Meanwhile, he passes us by in the opposite direction,

dancing endlessly.

Ernesto González © 2025

INTO THE WATERFALL

---∞---

Henry Henderson was out on yet another excursion of course with his trusty kayak, which had taken him on many great adventures. He was hoping this would be another magical journey like the ones in the past.

Henry was a true naturalist he would go on kayak tours for seasons on end, living off the land. Eating mainly fish, and food that grows wild, like berries, wild mushrooms, and herbs. Today he was travelling along a very rocky river. He had heard that there was a great waterfall, and he had been dying to see it. Since he heard the stories of its mystic beauty he decided then and there that would be his next trip! He had been gone for weeks, he did not have any care about how long it would take him, because he also was not sure.

He was told to look for the path where the river narrows into the middle of a forest between two islands. He was still in the wide-open blue; he could see two islands with a creek going between them. He stopped at the edge of the land and camped for the night. The falls were straight ahead of him from there. He also had a feeling he would be going against the current. Henry pulled his kayak up to the land; he slept under the open stars after a meal of the tasty food he had gathered.

He woke up at the crack of dawn to the sound of chirping birds. He packed up his gear and jumped into his kayak. He headed down the narrow stoney creek that he hoped would take him to the beauty of a site, and that it did. He travelled the morning hours into the afternoon.

He could hear rushing water, and the creek started to widen. Eventually he could see the mists coming off the white water that rushed into a pool ahead of him beneath a magnificent waterfall incased in an incredible stone surface.

Henry planned to get as close as he could to the pool then he would get out and portage up the hill and come out to the other side. He got to the point where the water was rippling under his kayak; he decided it was time to get out and start his hike. As he started to change course, the water started splashing and waving pulling him inward. With the way the current flew it should have been pushing him back, but the waves started pulling him in. He attempted to use his skill to pull himself out until the water claimed him.

The tide pulled him into the pool of waves he kept himself afloat then the fear struck in when he realized he was headed straight toward the stone surface of the stone wall beneath the falls. One last wave crashed into him hard; he prepared for this to be the end of his adventures. He shut his eyes and let out a bloody scream until he felt a deep calm over him and an aroma of salt, he was in an open blue body of water.

Once he realized he was safe he eased his guard and started to paddle again. The water was a still calm, the sun was shining reflecting on the open blue, he kept travelling straight for hours. Ahead of him Henry started to see islands and land, it was glowing! Already amazed at the site he started to hear a sound which lingered him in toward the magnificent song of what seemed to be an angel. He started paddling quicker the sound grew stronger, and the site of the islands grew closer until he arrived. He stopped his kayak as he was welcomed by creatures he had never seen anything like them before. There were four mermaids all with long dark hair, and wild eyes as sharp as nails.

Above them flew what looked like a mermaid, but there were wings on her back; she was the one that had been singing the song to attract Henry. He was breathless when he laid his eyes on the goddesses.

"Hello Henry" the flying siren said. The mermaids giggled then she continued "Henry our people are being taken out by killer whales, they took over our home at the bottom of the ocean. There was a shipwreck where we were staying, that is until they kicked us out and tried to destroy all of us!! Mr. Henry we are begging you for your help, we know of your past adventures and how you throw like no one else."

"Yes, Henry we need your help" One of the mermaids pleaded helplessly, "You're the only man for the job."

The rest of the mermaids chimed in, "yes Henry we need your help!"

Henry seemed confused yet very intrigued, especially by the beauty of the creatures. "Well how do you beautiful ladies expect me to help?" He asked.

"We have a special tool and if the rumors are correct, you are the one true master of throwing. I have heard you are the greatest axe thrower around, am I correct Mr. Henderson?"

"Well, it sounds like you have some pretty good sources," Henry said. "Do you have a silver axe for me to throw?"

"This time it is a little different." The flying siren started twirling her hair and continued her manipulation games. "Not exactly an axe Mr. Henderson it is a trident. This time a gold one and you are the only man who is strong and skilled enough to handle it." The flying siren spoke to him in a strong voice that brought chills, it was very manipulating, charming, and fierce all at the same time.

"A trident you say?"

"Yes, Henry it is part of our lost treasure. The killer whales have the rest of it hidden and they plan to do awful things with the powers they hold. Henry, everyone knows about your previous adventures. That is why you were brought you here, to help us."

"What kind of powers?"

"Oh, you are such a curious boy aren't you; now will you help us?"

"Me killing killer whales? I do not know if this is an adventure I want to go on."

"Henry, I think I can convince you." His eyes darted at her then she flew directly at him, kissing him in a fierce heavy way. When she was done, Henry had a new thought process. He had it in his head to kill the killer whales for the flying siren and her beautiful mermaids.

The serpents led the way to where the treasure was located. The flying siren firmly said "stop!!" and Henry listened to her command; his eyes were swirling he was willing to do whatever she wanted.

"Henry dear I need you to dive down there and take out the killer whales with the trident."

Two of the mermaids swam over carrying the trident together. Henry reached out to grab it and one of the mermaids stated, "here you go Mr. Henderson, do us proud." The mermaids told him nicely.

"Now go!" the siren demanded.

Henry jumped out of his kayak and dived deep down into the ocean blue he found himself having a new swimming ability, he was fast as a shark. He also noticed that his lungs were not bothering him, in his mind he really was not thinking at all. His brain was completely under her control.

He kept swimming until he seen the shipwreck; the water looked so clear that he saw them. The true creatures of beauty guarding the shipwreck. They were just minding their own business. Henry heard the siren's voice telling him what to do. He eyed the target, caulked his arm, and fired. The trident went straight towards his target.

Then all a sudden a weird creature with horns like an antelope, giant feet like a rabbit slammed the trident down before it could hit the heavy mammal.

The killer whales were now charging at Henry. He tried to flee; he looked around and noticed that he was now surrounded. He did not know what to do. Yet again he thought his adventures were over for good.

All a sudden a familiar face and figure popped up Infront of him, a light shined the figure revealed himself it was Jack the Jackalope. A beast Henry met on a previous adventure; Jack was a large rabbit with the horns of an antelope he was known as a Jackelope that could stand, walk, and talk.

"Henry" he said. "You must snap out of this." Henry then realized the situation he was in. Jack continued "Henry you have been tricked my child. I have come from my homeland as a spirt guide. I brought you here to destroy those retched serpents. Henry you must take the golden trident and stick it through the heart of the flying siren; she is the monster you must stop!!"

Henry looked over toward the sunken ship. "There she is!!!!" Henry exclaimed.

"Henry my child now you must do what you were sent here to do." The great Jackalope looked to the killer whales that were still swarming them. He said, "gentlemen let my friend here pass and he will take care of that awful harpy. Now Henry go get that trident and stop it before one of those dreaded mermaids gets to it first!"

Henry looked across staring at the shiny golden weapon peeking out of the coral ground. He jolted over there with the speed of a shark. As he did this the mermaids caught a glimpse of him as they were on their way to the shipwreck to get the riches they desired.

The siren took notice of what Henry was after and screamed a shrill cry, "get him!!" The mermaids stormed towards him it was at this time they showed their true faces. They were ugly creatures with white eyes, vicious yellow fangs, and tattered hair. They were no longer the beautiful mystical mermaids; they were now revealed as the true serpents they were.

The chase for the trident was on. Good versus bad, right versus wrong, man versus fish. Not only that but a battle of speed and inner strength, and heart something Henry was full of. He gave it everything he had. Then finally he got his hands on the treasure he pulled it from the ground. The hideous serpents grabbed him they took him down. Again, Henry thought this would be the end of his adventures. Henry fought against the monsters they tried to tear the treasure from his hands the mermaids swarmed above him. The siren laughing. That is until Henry gave it one more fight, his last stand.

Henry really struggled to get up right to swim, he fought hard, he caulked his arm back one more time with force. He swung forward throwing the gold trident, it landed straight into the chest of the hideous serpent.

By the time it hit her the mermaids were on top of Henry attempting to rip the flesh and life away from him. As soon as the trident struck her, she let out an awful scream. A terrible cry, this was by far the worst noise Henry had ever heard. Then a flash of dark light that pulsed through the water Henry let out a cry, he knew his adventure was over.

Suddenly Henry felt at peace. He felt fresh air upon him, and misty water splashing at him. He had a sense of adrenaline, he opened his eyes, he woke up from his nightmare and was living his dream.

He looked ahead and seen he was about to approach a giant waterfall he was in his trusty kayak ready to take on a real challenge. He paddled and paddled; he went straight down the giant cliff he landed with a giant splash and a joyful happy hauler. Henry got caught in the tide, he started going down a ripple of rapids and a series of waterfalls, this was his ultimate dream.

After an hour of struggling to survive he came out into a clear river, and he let out a loud cheer of excitement and joy. Henry did not know much about what just happened, but he knew he just went on one heck of a trip. The best adventure of his life.

For now,

Jesse Calnan © 2025

ABOUT THE AUTHORS

MARIELA IVÓN ARMANDO

Mariela Ivón Armando is a seasoned English and Spanish teacher with a master's degree in editing and editorial management from Argentina.

At 37, she not only excels in the classroom but also leads Connect Book Services, a company she founded to assist authors globally with editing, publishing, and the promotion of books.

Although Mariela started writing stories at the age of 12, she stepped into the literary world as an author in February 2022 with her self-published book, "El Lado Oscuro."

Additionally, her creative prowess is showcased in several tales published by Editorial Rubin in different anthologies throughout 2023, with two more stories set to be featured in an upcoming anthology in 2024.

Mariela's multifaceted career highlights her dedication to both education and the enriching world of literature.

PETER DRAPER

Peter Draper was born in Northfleet, Kent in the UK and grew up in the area. Following a very brief stint in the military he had a variety of jobs that eventually took him to America and Canada.

In 1995 he took up skydiving and very quickly became an instructor and certificated parachute rigger, a skill that he took to a major parachute equipment manufacturing company. He eventually racked up over 7,000 jumps, many as a tandem instructor taking people on their first ever skydives.

This in turn led to working with the Qatar Armed Forces where for over 10 years he worked for the Qatar Joint Special Forces (Airborne) until his retirement in 2020. During his time in Qatar, he trained with many elite groups from around the world including the Italian Folgare and the French Foreign Legion amongst others. He now lives in The Philippines with his wife Veronica.

Author's website: https://sites.google.com/view/peter-draper/home

DAMIAN NAKARE II

Damian Nakare II grew up in poverty in the ghetto. He was helpless, and his handicap made his childhood hard. Bullies targeted him at school and in the community.

Many people tease him with funny names. But his mother encouraged him to be strong. At age 24, he believed in the Lord Jesus.

He accepted the gospel of grace. He is passionate about preaching and teaching the Bible. He also offers guidance to those going through hard times. He spreads the good news of our Lord Jesus Christ to others. He hopes to work with God, the Creator of Heaven.

His book is 'The Gospel in Seven Words: clarifying John 3:16.' In this book, he offers a concise summary of the grace-based gospel

SAI MARIE JOHNSON

Sai Marie Johnson is an Oregon novelist, independent journalist, and freelance designer with over a decade's worth of experience.

She has worked with NYT, USA Today, and Amazon's bestselling authors in addition to providing consulting on author services, public relations, marketing, and branding.

A passionate activist and author Sai Marie Johnson has dedicated her life to the advocacy of important issues such as social justice, racism, sexism, human trafficking and genetic research for Duchenne's Muscular dystrophy.

Author's website: https://saimariejohnson.wordpress.com/

W. D. KILPACK III

W.D. Kilpack III is an award-winning and critically acclaimed internationally published writer, with works appearing in print, online, radio and television, starting with his first publication credit at the age of nine, when he wrote an award-winning poem. As an adult, his first two novels, Crown Prince and Order of Light, both received the Firebird Book Award, while Crown Prince received The BookFest Award. He also received special recognition from L. Ron Hubbard's Writers of the Future Contest for his novella, Pale Face.

Kilpack has been editor and/or publisher of 19 news and literary publications, both online and in print, with circulations as high as 770,000. He is an accomplished cook and has two claims he thinks few can match: cooking nearly every type of food on a grill; and nearly being knocked flat when his grill exploded.

Author's website: https://www.kilpack.net/

MICHAEL WHYATT BROOKES

The author has been an RAF officer, the Deputy Director of a regional local government body, and co-partner in a company offering management development and leadership training.

He has lived in England, France, Cyprus and Nigeria and has generally travelled widely. Past interests have included mountaineering, flying, gliding, skiing and motorcycling. Now he writes, paints, learns Italian, improves his French and keeps fit in a local gym and swimming pool.

Author's website: https://michaelwhyattbrookes.com/

JESSE CALNAN

Jesse Calnan is a budding author with a passion for weaving captivating tales.

"Way of the Ghosts," his debut collection of short stories, explores the mysterious and the richness of the people he writes about.

He spends his free time devouring as many books as possible to enrich his own writing.

He is currently working on a fantasy series, that focuses on a magic land with many original characters and creatures. He had the idea for a decade and fooled around with different thoughts.

Now he is committed to working on it and hopes to have the first book released some point this year of 2024.

GRIZZLY G. GUS

Grizzly G. Gus is a good ole boy, and he is M. David Lutz's cousin, a famous author (or so says M. David Lutz).

Grizzly lives in a double-wide mobile home in a senior citizens' park, in Florida, now retired from the Navy and Civil Service. He spends his day (besides drinking) saying and doing things none of us would. Grizzly's works are more edgy, certainly not PG. However, Lutz pointed out an interesting point.

He stated that when Grizzly was submitting his short stories and he was doing the same to various magazines, Grizzly got published while Lutz did not.

Grizzly is happy to state that his success was such because he hired his cousin M. David Lutz to be his publisher. As his publisher, M. David Lutz is tasked with toning down Grizzly's short stories for projects, in addition to all the other requirements for publishing. Leaving Grizzly with the task of staying sober enough to write.

Grizzly has a ton of short stories.

As far as social media, Grizzly has:

His own email: grizzlyggus@outlook.com

His own Facebook page: https://fb.com/grizzlyggus

However, since he is lazy, Grizzly shares M. David Lutz's website: http://www.mdavidlutz.com

One last note: My specialty is short stories, blogs, and an advice column. No matter how I beg, my cousin feels I need more of a following before he commits to helping me publish my first book.

That is my cousin M. David Lutz.

CURTIS L. L. HERBOLD

When I started writing, I was not the best person with language skills, the fancy car, the money, or anything else of value. I never even dreamed of being a "Best Selling" author. I am just living my own life, on my own in a one-bedroom apartment, minimum wage part time job, and paying my dues to society, but I did this without the help of family, friends, or government officials like caseworkers. The only help I had was to get my first book edited professionally by a freelance editor. To start my journey, I wrote the plot, the story, and everything about the book and its series; I wrote this whole web page, the tools, the covers, and my Facebook page for my series. Everything you see is a-well I guess you could say it's an image of me, since I have done it all. Even if I do not become rich and famous of the series, at least I get to say I did this, and I am proud of myself for accomplishing what I have, especially considering the challenges that I have had.

Author's website:

https://www.thedetectivecurtischronicles.net/

M. GARNET

Muriel G. Yantiss writes under the pen name M. Garnet.

Her time owning an International Business gave her a hard view of life, but her farm family in Kentucky left her with a great sense of humour to enjoy everything, bad and good.

Writing has allowed her to put these observations down and share them with others, lacing each story with facts.

Living now in Florida with her daughter and son in law, a dog and two cats and a quaker parrot she still ends most letters with her statement: life is good.

She has published many books so look for her other titles.

Author's website: https://www.mgarnet.com/

DR ROBIN CRAIG

Dr Robin Craig is a scientist and philosopher who enjoys writing dramatic and engaging stories driven by strong characters and intriguing philosophical themes: stories you love to read that make you think.

His main subjects are near future science fiction exploring contemporary issues like artificial intelligence and human genetic engineering, but other themes include time travel, historical fiction, fantasy and short stories.

Author's website: https://robin-craig.com/bio/#author

SARAH DESOUZA

Sarah Desouza lives in the sun-soaked shores of Goa, India, where she crafts relatable short stories on her Medium blog. With a passion for storytelling, Sarah aims for her narratives to leave a lasting impression, imparting valuable lessons to her readers.

Frequently infused with Christian themes and moral reflections, her tales delve into the depths of human experience. Sarah's writing transcends abstract concepts, rendering them palpable, particularly in explorations of love and the divine.

Among her literary endeavors is the book 'His Lingering Perfume,' available on Amazon. For Sarah, writing is not just a hobby but a means of self-expression. She finds solace in creating worlds where beauty and perfection intertwine, only to find deeper meaning through the lens of faith in her stories.

M. DAVID LUTZ

M. (Mark) David Lutz is a dedicated writer, specializing in comedy and satire. He started seriously writing humor over twenty years ago. Primarily publishing articles and short stories until he turned his attention to writing a book series.

He has assisted other writers, encouraging them to develop their talents and helping them publish their projects.

Retiring after forty years of government service, Mark looks forward to writing full-time.

He regularly communicates with readers through his website and Facebook accounts while continuing to write additional volumes to his 'Princess and Plumber' series in addition to other projects. He currently resides overseas with his wife and daughter.

Author's website: http://www.mdavidlutz.com/index.html

PETER MCCOLLUM

Peter McCollum is an ESL tutor and writing professor who recently stepped away from the classroom to pursue his dream of getting his stories published.

He is an avid gardener, boasting about several surviving plants and trees.

Peter is also a music fanatic and will try his best to corner you and make you listen to something. Please be warned.

An expatriate of 11 years, Peter lives in sunny Thailand with his wife, Nim, his daughter, Leia, and his cats, Anakin and Padme.

THE PAPER MAN

A South-African born Australian Poet, The Paper Man has written over 1000 poems in 1000 days.

With stories that range from subjects such as parenthood, love, loss, the funny and heartwarming, his poetry guarantees to have something for everyone.

With his first book "The Paper Man's Tales" available now, he plans to continue writing and hopes to delve into the world of voiceovers as he has brought life to the many characters that he has created.

Author's website: https://thepapermanpoems.com/

ERNESTO GONZALEZ

Ernesto González, a Cuban writer, holds a degree in Scientific Information and is the author of several novels. He has published poems, short stories, and articles in digital and Chicago media outlets.

He served as an advisor for the Spanish Proficiency Test created by Riverside Publishing. He worked as a Spanish professor at East-West University and the Cultural Exchange language academy, and for thirteen years as a translator for the Chicago Tribune's Hoy newspaper.

His novels are available on Amazon.com.

José F. Nodar

The Cuban revolution in 1959 presented José with one of his many life challenges. José was born in La Habana; Cuba, and the Cuban revolution saw him get on a plane alone at eleven years of age and arrive at an orphanage in the small town of Washington, Georgia. He did not get to see his parents again until he was eighteen years old and had graduated from high school in Atlanta, Georgia.

He studied Business Administration at Georgia State University. From university, he headed into the finance world working for the First National Bank of Atlanta (now Wells Fargo) and then moved into the financial consulting world working as a project manager, travelling to many assignments in the United States, Europe, and Australia.

José began writing his debut novel after getting his feet wet in creative writing at a writers' group in Camden, New South Wales, Australia. This gave him 'the bug' as he calls it and soon his mind created his first major character, Danny Monk.

Currently, José is working on his twelfth collection of short stories and poetry and several romantic novels due out later in the year.

He is also working on a tribute book to his wonderful wife and muse, Miriam Vassallo Nodar, who sadly passed away on June 10, 2025.

When José is not writing, you can find him sitting at the local shopping mall watching people and getting inspiration for his future characters.

When not in front of his computer working away, José is reading or spending leisurely walks around the Spring Farm area.

Author's website: https://www.jfnodar.com.au/

www.ingramcontent.com/pod-product-compliance
Lightning Source LLC
Chambersburg PA
CBHW061728070526
44583CB00024B/3045